MW00411993

OUR
WITNESS *to*
the WORLD

THE KINGDOM PASTOR'S LIBRARY

OUR WITNESS to the WORLD

Equipping the Church for
Evangelism and Social Impact

TONY EVANS

MOODY PUBLISHERS

CHICAGO

Content in this book is adapted from *One Church Under God* (Chicago: Moody Publishers, 2014), The Urban Alternative (various flyers), *Oneness Embraced* (Chicago: Moody Publishers, 2015), *God's Glorious Church* (Chicago: Moody Publishers, 2004), and the Tony Evans Training Center.

All Scripture quotations, unless otherwise indicated, are taken from the New American Standard Bible®, Copyright © 1960, 1962, 1963, 1968, 1971, 1972, 1973, 1975, 1977, 1995 by The Lockman Foundation. Used by permission. www.Lockman.org

Scripture quotations marked NIV are taken from the Holy Bible, New International Version®, NIV®. Copyright © 1973, 1978, 1984, 2011 by Biblica, Inc.™ Used by permission of Zondervan. All rights reserved worldwide. www.zondervan.com. The "NIV" and "New International Version" are trademarks registered in the United States Patent and Trademark Office by Biblica, Inc.™

Scripture quotations marked KJV are taken from the King James Version.

Edited by Michelle Sincock
Interior Design: Erik M. Peterson
Cover Design: Thinkpen Design
Cover photo of wheat field copyright © 2019 by Ievgenii Meyer / Shutterstock (663208498). All rights reserved.

All websites and phone numbers listed herein are accurate at the time of publication but may change in the future or cease to exist. The listing of website references and resources does not imply publisher endorsement of the site's entire contents. Groups and organizations are listed for informational purposes, and listing does not imply publisher endorsement of their activities.

Library of Congress Cataloging-in-Publication Data

Names: Evans, Tony, 1949- author.
Title: Our witness to the world : equipping the church for evangelism and
   social impact / Dr. Tony Evans.
Description: Chicago : Moody Publishers, 2020. | Series: The kingdom
   pastor's library | Includes bibliographical references. | Summary: "Our
   Witness to the World is the latest book in Kingdom Pastor's Library, a
   new series of books that brings you a succinct, complete pastoral
   philosophy and training from Tony Evans. Look for its release in 2020 or
   pre-order now"-- Provided by publisher.
Identifiers: LCCN 2019036434 (print) | LCCN 2019036435 (ebook) | ISBN
   9780802418333 (hardcover) | ISBN 9780802496928 (ebook)
Subjects: LCSH: Spiritual formation. | Influence--Religious
   aspects--Christianity. | Christianity and culture. | Evangelistic work.
Classification: LCC BV4511 .E93 2020 (print) | LCC BV4511 (ebook) | DDC
   269--dc23
LC record available at https://lccn.loc.gov/2019036434

Originally delivered by fleets of horse-drawn wagons, the affordable paperbacks from D. L. Moody's publishing house resourced the church and served everyday people. Now, after more than 125 years of publishing and ministry, Moody Publishers' mission remains the same—even if our delivery systems have changed a bit. For more information on other books (and resources) created from a biblical perspective, go to www.moodypublishers.com or write to:

Moody Publishers
820 N. LaSalle Boulevard
Chicago, IL 60610

1 3 5 7 9 10 8 6 4 2

Printed in the United States of America

CONTENTS

PART ONE

EVANGELISM

CHAPTER ONE

THE PURPOSE

———————————— ◆ ————————————

When you see the mainstream culture deteriorating, look closer, and you will probably see a people of God who have withdrawn from the culture and turned it over to the unrighteous to rule. A divided culture can only reflect one thing: a divided church. And by "divided," I'm not just talking about division along racial, cultural or class lines. Unfortunately, the division looms much larger than that. In our post-modern culture today, we are often divided on doctrine, mission, vision, and outreach as well. Consider:

- Over half of all Americans believe Jesus sinned while on earth (52%)[1]

———————————

1. "What Do Americans Believe about Jesus? 5 Popular Beliefs," Barna, April 1, 2015, https://www.barna.com/research/what-do-americans-believe-about-jesus-5-popular-beliefs/.

- Nearly half (47%) of Christian Millennials (those born in 1984–1988) agree that "it is wrong to share one's personal beliefs with someone of a different faith in hopes that they will one day share the same faith."[2]
- 52% of US Protestants believe that faith alone is not enough for salvation, but rather ascribe to faith and good works as the way into heaven.[3]

I could go on with these alarming realities, but I think you get the picture: we have lost our way within the church. Granted, polls and studies do leave room for subjective interpretations and other studies performed by groups outside of Barna and Pew (quoted above) have not landed on as dismal of results. But even though they may not be *as* dismal, they are revealing a Christian culture at a collective loss for doctrinal truth.

God's people have been called to influence society. Unfortunately, with our shift in emphasis to seeker-sensitive, prosperity-promoting, sin-marginalizing, entertainment-experiencing churches, that influence may not always be a good thing. What we need now—from our kingdom-minded

---

2. "Almost Half of Practicing Christian Millennials Say Evangelism Is Wrong," Barna, February 5, 2019, https://www.barna.com/research/millennials-oppose-evangelism/.

3. "U.S. Protestants Are Not Defined by Reformation-Era Controversies 500 Years Later," Pew Research Center, August 31, 2017, https://www.pewforum.org/2017/08/31/u-s-protestants-are-not-defined-by-reformation-era-controversies-500-years-later/. Eighty-one percent of Catholics believe the same.

pastors and church leaders is a return to the fundamentals of the faith. If we are going to carry out the commission of our Lord and Savior Jesus Christ to impact culture for good, we must return to a focus on evangelism and discipleship that results in spiritual and social transformation.

Discipleship is that *developmental process that progressively brings Christians from spiritual infancy to spiritual maturity so that they are then able to reproduce the process with someone else.* The singular, overarching goal of a disciple is to bring all of life under the lordship of Jesus Christ and then help someone else to do the same.

Yet, you cannot make disciples out of the lost. The nations are not told to come to Christians for the gospel. We need to go to them. The church is not doing the work of the church if we are not winning souls to Christ. We must keep evangelism (with the goal of making disciples) front and center in the life of the church. If the church is going to grow by making disciples, we have to have people who are willing to go into the whole world as Christ's kingdom witnesses.

Evangelism is defined as *sharing the good news of Christ's substitutionary death and resurrection and His free offer of forgiveness for sin and eternal life to all who, by faith, come to Him to receive it.* Evangelism and making disciples is done with the clear intent of bringing the hearer to faith in Jesus Christ for salvation. People must be born from above into the kingdom before they can be developed into disciples of the kingdom. The church, then, must challenge, encourage, and equip its members to effectively share their faith with unbelievers. Your role as a pastor involves both inspiring and preparing your flock for evangelism and making disciples, in addition to your own evangelizing through your preaching, teaching, and in your personal relationships.

Entire books have been written on the church's mission, but perhaps the most comprehensive summary of our calling is the text commonly called the Great Commission (see Matt. 28:16–20). This Great Commission summarizes the twofold mission of the church which is to evangelize (lead people into the kingdom) and disciple (develop believers to become full-time Christ followers). These are some of the last words of Jesus Christ before His ascension to heaven, which makes them crucial for that reason alone. But these are also very important words because they contain Christ's final instructions to His church.

Jesus articulated the church's mission when He met with His followers in Galilee after the resurrection (see Mark 16:7). Matthew 28:16 says, "The eleven disciples proceeded to Galilee, to the mountain which Jesus had designated." This was the only organized meeting He called during the forty days He was on earth between His resurrection and ascension. There were actually three groups at this meeting, including the eleven apostles (Judas was dead) and a second group that Paul called the "more than five hundred brethren" who saw the risen Christ at the same time (1 Cor. 15:6).

The third group at this all-important meeting was there in spirit. This includes all believers from that day until Jesus comes again. How do I know we are part of the Great Commission meeting? Because Jesus said His commission to make disciples is in effect "even to the end of the age" (Matt. 28:20), which hasn't come yet. So the Lord's instructions are for us as pastors and church leaders and our congregants.

WE MUST GO

Jesus began His proclamation to us with these words: "*Go* therefore and make disciples of all the nations, *baptizing* them in the name of the Father and the Son and the Holy Spirit, *teaching* them to observe all that I commanded you; and lo, I am with you always, even to the end of the age" (Matt. 28:19–20). Notice that we are not just discipling individuals, but whole people groups, which includes influencing the social, political, and economic systems that affect their lives.

The first of the three things we need to do in our evangelistic mission is to be intentional in evangelism in our everyday lives. Jesus' Great Commission blends both evangelism and discipleship in order to impact a person holistically. It begins with evangelism; however, once a person trusts in Christ for salvation, then the next phase involves discipleship. Both are to be carried out as we go about our everyday lives. The idea here is, "As you go, make disciples." In other words, Jesus expects us to be going out. We could even say that our going is assumed. What we are talking about is the ministry of evangelism.

WE MUST BAPTIZE

Jesus said that another part of this charge is baptizing those who have accepted Christ. He was not telling us simply to get people wet. The problem in too many cases is that people go into baptism as dry sinners and come out as wet ones. There is much more to baptism than just undergoing a ritual involving water.

In fact, the primary theological meaning of the Greek word for baptism is "identification." This was a very picturesque word in New Testament days. It was used of dipping a cloth into a dye so that the cloth became completely identified with the dye by absorbing its color. The cloth was immersed in the dye until it took on the character of the dye. The cloth underwent a complete identity change.

This is the picture behind Romans 6:3–4, where Paul wrote,

> Do you not know that all of us who have been baptized into Christ Jesus have been baptized into His death? Therefore we have been buried with Him

through baptism into death, so that as Christ was
raised from the dead through the glory of the Father,
so we too might walk in newness of life.

When we put our trust in Christ, we became so completely
identified with Him that His death and resurrection to new
life became our death and resurrection. When we immerse
believers in the waters of baptism, we are picturing their
death to the old life and resurrection to a new way of life.
That happened the moment they trusted Christ, but the ordi-
nance of water baptism was given to the church as an outward
testimony to this inward change. It is a public declaration of
a person's personal conversion, as well as a willingness to be
publicly identified as a visible, verbal follower of Christ. Baptism, then, is related to discipleship and not just conversion.

Many Christians struggle in their daily lives because they
don't understand their new identity. They don't know who
they are in Christ. You see, our identity used to be in Adam,
but not anymore. We have to realize that being "in Christ"
is such a radically new way of life that whatever happens to
Christ happens to us. That's why the Bible says that when
Christ died we died, and when Christ arose from the dead we
arose. Now that we are in Christ, we have been accepted by
God. We don't have to try to make God like us. So, if you're
on a performance treadmill in your Christian life trying to

do all the right things and keep God happy with you, get off that thing and start living like someone who is identified with Christ and accepted by Him. Christ must be the reference point for both our decisions and our actions.

It's like putting a letter in an envelope and sealing it shut. When I do that, I don't have to ask where the letter is because the letter is safely sealed inside the envelope. So wherever the envelope goes, the letter will go too—and it's against the law for anyone but the recipient of that sealed envelope to break that seal.

Christ is the envelope, and we are the letter. We are *in Christ.* The Bible says that when you believed on Jesus Christ "you were sealed in Him with the Holy Spirit of promise" (Eph. 1:13). How do I know I am going to heaven? Not because I'm a preacher, but because I am in Christ, and He is already seated at the right hand of the Father in heaven. I am linked with Christ forever by virtue of His grace in saving, sealing, and keeping me.

WE MUST TEACH

Once people have believed the gospel and have been identified with Christ, we must teach them "to observe all that I commanded you" (Matt. 28:20). As a church leader, I am sure you can really get into this one. But teaching the nations involves more than teaching them theology, Christology, soteriology, and all the other "ologies" of the faith. Jesus said the goal is that people "observe" or *obey* all that He commanded us. Of course, our teaching must have solid content, because Christians are people of the truth and people of the Book. Jesus' commands that we are to obey are contained in the Word. But the goal is not content alone. The goal of biblical teaching is to combine information and knowledge with skill in applying the truth to daily life.

That's why, for example, after Jesus fed four thousand people, He "immediately" had His disciples get into a boat and head out (see Mark 8:1–10). According to Mark 8:14–21, Jesus wanted them to apply the lesson they had just learned about His power to meet their needs. There wasn't enough food on board for the group, and the disciples were trying to figure out what they were going to eat. So Jesus asked them some pointed questions that ended with, "Do you not yet understand?" (v. 21). Obviously they didn't, but you can be sure they thought about it for a long time and eventually the message got through.

WRAPPING IT UP

Our witness to the world starts with evangelism and carries on through the process of discipleship in promoting personal spiritual development. It is not only handing out a tract or giving a Gospel message. We limit our effectiveness in carrying out Christ's commission when we fail to understand the holistic nature of evangelism, including both the scope and content of the Gospel.

Evangelism, done rightly, is no easy thing. That's why Jesus closed the Great Commission with a tremendous promise of His presence (see Matt. 28:20). As the Lord of the church, Jesus promises us an even greater opportunity to witness His abiding presence and power to carry out His commission. This is more than a promise of Christ's presence with us as individual believers to deal with situations in our daily lives, although of course He is always with us and His authority and presence remain with us due to His promise "I am with you always" (Matt. 28:20). This is Christ's authority given to the church to make disciples of all the nations. But to position our congregants to witness the firsthand experience of God's authority and presence, we have to inspire and prepare our congregants to be more than just pew-sitters or attenders when it comes to the church and its ministry.

Jesus' promise in the context of the Great Commission means that when local churches are doing what He commanded, they are going to have a greater ability to witness the full manifestation of his working presence and power in answer to prayer that they wouldn't have otherwise. They are going to tap into the offered authority in ministry Jesus has promised. They are going to see God show up in ways that go beyond the normal and expected. Conversely, Jesus lessens the visual demonstration of His authoritative presence when discipleship is missing (see John 2:23–25).

This promise is so incredible that if we're not seeing this kind of kingdom authority and power being exercised in the church, we need to ask ourselves why. When the church is committed to the mission of making disciples, initiated by evangelism, we have Jesus' permission to use His name, His authority, His rights, and His privileges. That's all we will ever need to accomplish the church's kingdom assignment.

CHAPTER TWO

THE PATH

———————— ◆ ————————

When famed NFL coach Vince Lombardi stood before his team and said, "This is a football," most of the players wondered what he was talking about. Of course that was a football. These were professional football players, after all. Yet this reality did not deter Coach Lombardi from seeking to remind them of the basics. In doing so, he took them back to the fundamentals of the game. As a result, he also took them forward into years of championship playing down the road.

As a pastor, you may feel that this chapter is not for you. You may also feel that it does not belong near the front of a book written for pastors and church leaders. But after seeing the statistics that show 52% of US Protestants believe that salvation is based on faith *plus* works, I'm concerned that some of our pastors may not be clear on salvation either, let alone how to present the gospel. So to return to the fundamentals of our faith, let's review what has been known as the Romans Road.[1]

The outline I am using is not original to me. You may already know it. I did not discover it; I simply expanded upon it. However, I've found it simple to remember and easy to use, and I believe it's worth our time revisiting. By using key passages from the book of Romans, we can outline everything a man or woman needs to know in order to receive eternal life in Jesus Christ.

THE PROBLEM

For all have sinned and fall short of the glory of God.
Romans 3:23

Salvation is *good news,* but it comes to us against a backdrop of bad news. The bad news is this: we are all sinners. Not one man or woman on planet earth—past, present or future—is without sin.

The Greek word for "sin" literally means to "miss the mark." It's like a bowman who drew back his string, released his arrow,

---

1. Multiple ways of understanding and presenting the gospel message exist. The Romans Road is just one. You may also want to explore other methods not only for yourself, but as tools for equipping your church members to both understand and share the gospel themselves: www.tonyevans.org/witness.

but failed to hit the bull's-eye. Similarly, sin involves missing the target. What is the target? The verse we just looked at tells us: "All have sinned and *fall short of the glory of God.*" Sin is falling short of God's glory—His standard of perfection.

To help you understand this concept, I must attack a popular myth maintained by the media, the literary community, and sometimes even the church itself. The fable is that sin can be measured by degree. For many of us, criminals seem like big-time sinners, while those of us who tell little white lies are lightweight sinners. It appears logical to believe that those in county jail have not sinned as seriously as those in the state penitentiary. But sin looks quite different from God's perspective.

In Scripture, sin is not measured by degree. Either we fall short of God's glory or we don't. Since the entire sin question pivots on this point, let's make sure we understand our target. The word "glory" means to put something on display—to show it off. Sin is missing the mark, and the mark is to properly "put God on display." When we view the issue from this perspective, our understanding of sin begins to change. Any time we have ever done anything that did not reveal who and what God is accurately, any time we fail to reflect the character of God, then we have sinned.

The story is told of two men who were exploring an island when, suddenly, a volcano erupted. In moments, the two found themselves surrounded by molten lava. Several feet away was a clearing and a path to safety. To get there, however, they would have to jump across the river of melted rock. The first gentleman was an active senior citizen, but hardly an outstanding physical specimen. He ran as fast as he could, took an admirable leap, but traveled only a few feet. He met a swift death in the super-heated lava.

The other explorer was a much younger man in excellent physical condition. In fact, the college record he set in the broad jump had remained unbroken to that day. He put all his energy into his run, jumped with flawless form, and shattered his own college record. Unfortunately, he landed just short of the clearing. Though the younger man clearly out-performed his companion, both wound up equally dead. Survival was not reached, so ability became a non-issue.

Degrees of "goodness" may be important when hiring an employee or choosing neighbors. But when the issue is sin, the only standard that matters is God's perfect holiness. The question is not how you measure up against the guy down the street, but how you measure up to God. God's standard is perfect righteousness, and it is a standard that even the best behaved or most morally upright person still cannot reach. Unless you are as good as God, then you are a sinner who needs to be delivered from God's just wrath against sin.

THE PENALTY

*Therefore, just as sin entered the world through one man,
and death through sin, and in this way death came to all people,
because all sinned.* Romans 5:12 NIV

Now, as you read this passage, you may be thinking, "If sin entered the world through one man (Adam), it isn't fair to punish the rest of us." Yet, death spread to all men because "all have sinned." We are not punished simply because Adam sinned, but because we inherited Adam's propensity to sin, and have sinned ourselves.

Have you ever noticed that you don't need to teach your children how to sin? Can you imagine sitting down with your child and saying, "Here's how to lie successfully" or "Let me show you how to be selfish"? Those things come naturally. Let me illustrate this another way. Have you ever seen an apple with a small hole in it? If you do, don't eat it. The presence of the hole suggests that there is a worm in there waiting for you.

Now, most people don't know how the worm managed to take up residence in that apple. They think he was slithering by one day when he decided to bore through the outer skin of the fruit and set up house inside. However, that is not what happens. Worms hatch from larvae dropped on the apple blossom. The blossom becomes a bud and the bud turns into fruit. The apple literally grows up around the unborn worm.

The hole is left when the worm hatches and digs his way out.

In the same way, the seed of sin is within each and every one of us at the moment of birth. Though it may take some time before the evidence of sin shows on the surface, it is there and eventually it makes its presence known.

Sin demands a penalty. That penalty, according to Scripture, is death. That means physical death (where the soul is separated from the body) and spiritual death (where the soul is eternally separated from God).

THE PROVISION

But God demonstrates his own love for us in this:
While we were still sinners, Christ died for us. Romans 5:8 NIV

Two very powerful words when put together are "but God." Those words can revolutionize any situation. "My marriage is falling apart. But God . . ." "My husband abandoned us and my children are out of control. But God . . ." "I have no job, no income and no future. But God . . ." God can restore any situation. He is bigger and more powerful than any life challenge or any predicament with or resulting from sin.

"I'm a sinner condemned to eternal separation from God. But God . . ." Those same words sum up the good news for each of us. Even while we were still sinners, God proved His love for us by sending Jesus Christ to die in our place.

How amazing that God would love us so deeply. We have certainly done nothing to deserve it. But the amazement deepens when you consider the significance of Jesus' sacrifice on Calvary.

Because not just anybody could die for the penalty of sin. You see, we all have sinned. So none of us could die to pay the penalty of sin for others or ourselves. We each have our own price to pay. Whoever would save us must be perfectly sinless.

Two brothers were playing in the woods one summer day when, almost without warning, a honeybee flew down and stung the older brother on the eyelid. He put his hands to his face and fell to the ground in pain. As the younger brother looked on in horror, the honeybee began buzzing around his head. Terrified, he began screaming, "The bee's going to get me!" The older brother, regaining his composure, said, "What are you talking about? That bee can't hurt you, she's already stung me."

The Bible tells us that this is precisely what happened on Calvary. God loves you so much that He sent His Son, Jesus, to take the "stinger of death" in your place on Calvary as your personal substitute. Jesus hung on the cross, not for his own sin, but for my sin and yours. Because Jesus Christ is without sin, His death paid the penalty for all of us.

How do we know that Jesus' death on the cross really took care of the sin problem? Because of what happened on that Sunday morning. When Mary Magdalene came to Jesus' tomb that morning, she couldn't find him. She saw someone and thought it was a gardener. She asked him where the Lord's body had been taken. When the gardener turned and removed his cloak, Mary gasped in amazement. It was Jesus (see John 20:11–18). In fact, according to 1 Corinthians 15:1–6, over five hundred people personally saw the risen Christ before He ascended into heaven.

I am a Christian today because the tomb is empty. If not for the resurrection, our faith would be empty and useless. As the Apostle Paul said, if Jesus were not raised, we should be the most pitied people on earth. But the fact is, Jesus *is* raised and has conquered death on our behalf (see 1 Cor. 15:12–20).

THE PARDON

Now to the one who works, his wage is not credited as a favor,
but as what is due. But to the one who does not work,
but believes in Him who justifies the ungodly,
his faith is credited as righteousness. Romans 4:4–5

For by grace you have been saved through faith;
and that not of yourselves, it is the gift of God; not as
a result of works, so that no one may boast. Ephesians 2:8–9

If good works could save anyone, there would have been no point in Jesus' death. But Jesus knew we couldn't pay sin's price and earn acceptance with a holy God. That's why His sacrifice was vital. In order for His sacrifice to secure our pardon, we must trust in Him for our salvation.

Believing *in* Jesus means a great deal more than believing *about* Jesus. Knowing the facts about His life and death is mere "head knowledge." Believing in Jesus means to personally trust, to have total confidence, to "rest your case" on Him and His substitutionary atonement on the cross.

Without knowing, you illustrate this concept every time you sit down. The moment you commit your weight to a chair, you have "believed in" that chair to hold you up. Most of us have so much faith in chairs that, despite our weight, we will readily place ourselves down without a second thought.

If a tinge of doubt creeps in, you might steady yourself by grabbing something with your hand or by keeping your legs beneath you, resting only part of your weight on the chair. That's what many people do with salvation. They're reasonably sure that Jesus is who He said He is. However, they "hedge their bet" by putting some of their trust in their efforts at good behavior, their church traditions, or anything else they can do. To do so is to reject the total sufficiency of Christ's saving work on the cross.

You must understand that if you depend on anything beyond Jesus for your salvation, then what you're really saying is that Jesus Christ, and His substitutionary atonement, is not enough. Salvation comes through committing the entire weight of your eternal destiny to Jesus Christ and what He did on the cross. A person's eternal destiny must rest solely in Christ alone, by God's grace and their faith (see Eph. 2:8). Salvation has to do only with whether you have placed absolute confidence in the person of Christ and His promise to freely give eternal life to all who believe in Him for it.

WRAPPING IT UP

Many interpretations of salvation exist in our current contemporary culture. People often get confused that salvation comes through being good enough or seeking to keep the Ten Commandments. Others feel it is a comparison game, and as long as they are better than the majority of others, they will get in. And yet others believe that since God is a God of love, He really isn't serious about sending anyone to hell for eternity. Even many Christians and pastors mix works with faith, bringing confusion and contradiction to the free offer of eternal life (see Rom. 3:24; Rev. 21:6; 22:17).

Thus, while we may all use the terminology such as "saved" or "salvation" or "getting into heaven," we may not all be referring to the same meanings of those terms. That's why as a pastor, it is your role to clarify these terms for your congregation. Not only do you need your congregants to understand what salvation truly is and how to obtain it through faith alone in Christ alone, but you also need to disciple your church members on how to present the gospel to others.

As we sink deeper and deeper into a Bible-illiterate culture, your job as a pastor or church leader in teaching what the Bible truly says becomes all the more important. I hope and pray that you will use the simplicity of the gospel presentation in this chapter to not only sharpen your own understanding of how to present the message of salvation, but also be used by you to teach others.

CHAPTER THREE

THE PROVOCATION

◆

In ancient times when a king first took possession of the throne, his reign needed to be officially announced to all the would-be citizens of his kingdom. This announcement was the Greek word *euangelion* (combining *eu* meaning "good" and *angellia* meaning "news" or "announcement").

This announcement was the "good news" that the king had defeated his rivals, establishing peace for the inhabitants of his kingdom. This is the historical context for the *euangelion* (the gospel)—it is the royal proclamation of the good news of a new ruler taking or reclaiming the throne. The king would send out heralds or ambassadors to proclaim this good news and let everyone know who was now in charge.

Paul and the other writers of the New Testament understood the gospel in light of this context. They drew from the larger story of Scripture that tells of a good creation or good kingdom gone bad because of the fall of humanity into rebellion against the true King and Creator of this world.

Yet instead of taking back His earthly kingdom by force, God chose the most powerful weapon of all to win back His fallen, broken earthly kingdom: love (see John 3:16). Instead of an army, He sent His Son, who gave His life to offer the path of securing the hearts of the King's people. The gospel announces this good news, that a solution to the powers of sin and death has been won by Christ's death and His resurrection breaks the power of death (see 1 Cor. 15:3–4). The good news is that Jesus has conquered sin and death, so that just "as in Adam all die, so also in Christ all will be made alive" (1 Cor. 15:22).

MOTIVATIONS FOR EVANGELISM

Each of us are called to be heralds and ambassadors announcing this good news of Christ's death and resurrection and inviting people to place their faith in what He has accomplished on their behalf. As pastors and church leaders, your call includes both evangelizing but also inspiring others to evangelize. At the heart of this inspiration must lie a motivation rooted in obedience to God's Word. These motivations are outlined for us by the Apostle Paul in 2 Corinthians 5. They are:

- Fear of the Lord
- New life granted in Christ
- Ministry of reconciliation
- Love for God and others

The brilliant theologian and apostle Paul was fundamentally a missionary. He spent all of his time introducing people to the faith and then establishing churches in which they could grow. Paul never strayed far from evangelism. He never lost sight of the importance of his witness and the fact that others should be influenced by the message of the gospel.

Our witness to the world ought to be a part of who we are. The reason I say that is because if evangelism is only something you *do*, it becomes a program. For Paul, evangelism was more of who he was. Because his life was so wrapped up in Jesus Christ, sharing about Him was natural to his being. It was his chief joy to proclaim the Gospel. In fact, if evangelism is not part of your Christian life, then you are living in disobedience as well as missing out on the joy of the Lord because evangelism brings the Lord joy which overflows to you.

The first motivation is the *fear of the Lord*. Paul tells us this in 2 Corinthians 5:9–11 where it says,

So we make it our goal to please him, whether we are at home in the body or away from it. For we must all appear before the judgment seat of Christ, so that each of us may receive what is due us for the things done while in the body, whether good or bad. Since, then, we know what it is to fear the Lord, we try to persuade others. (NIV)

Paul's fear of the Lord was a motivation for him to persuade others. Paul knew God was to be taken seriously. Thus, if you and I are going to take God seriously, we will do whatever is legitimately within our spheres of influence to make sure that when we stand before God on the judgment day, we tried to please God and persuade others toward salvation.

Paul knew that the fear of the Lord ought to motivate us to share the Gospel in order to give those who were headed to eternal death a chance to repent. We see this sentiment expressed in 1 Peter 4:17–18,

For *it is* time for judgment to begin with the household of God; and if *it begins* with us first, what *will be* the outcome for those who do not obey the gospel of God? And if it is with difficulty that the righteous is saved, what will become of the godless man and the sinner?

What Paul shared in this passage was his awareness that if saints could expect a day of judgment before God, how much worse off will the unsaved be?

Another motivation Paul expressed in 2 Corinthians 5 is the *new life granted in Christ*. We read about this in verse 17, "Therefore, if anyone is in Christ, the new creation has come: The old has gone, the new is here!" (NIV). The gospel changes a person's life. Scripture tells us when a man or woman comes to Christ, they become a new creation. God's power becomes infused in their new life. He transforms lives through salvation.

Thus, when you and I evangelize, or when you equip your congregants to evangelize, we are participating in bringing a person into the space of spiritual transformation. The gospel can revolutionize anyone who receives it with faith. It is powerful because Jesus' power, through the Holy Spirit, comes to live inside the person once they receive Him.

A third motivation for witnessing to the world is the *ministry of reconciliation*. 2 Corinthians 5:18–19 reads,

> Now all these things are from God, who reconciled us to Himself through Christ and gave us the ministry of reconciliation, namely, that God was in Christ reconciling the world to Himself, not counting their trespasses against them, and He has committed to us the word of reconciliation.

In fact, 2 Corinthians 6:1 goes on to call us "workers together" (KJV) with God in this ministry. God has stated that He has chosen not do this ministry of reconciliation by Himself, but that He wants to do this ministry with us. He has invited us to participate with Him in the drama of the ages.

Our ministry is to seek the reconciliation to God of those who are lost. Your job as a pastor is to minister reconciliation in order to bring people into harmony with God. But your congregants are also called to this same ministry. You are there to let them know this truth as well because far too many church members do not know they are ministers themselves. Yet they are ministers of Christ whose job is to reconcile people to God. In fact, we are all ambassadors of Christ.

Ambassadors are people sent on diplomatic missions from their home country. The ambassador represents his home country, and it is through his voice and his actions that the country to which he is sent receives the message sent by his home country. In the same way, we are ambassadors for Christ. What this means is that as "ambassadors for Christ" God is now making His appeal to a lost and dying world through you as a church leader and through the congregants you are responsible for shepherding. It is through your voice, actions, and teaching that the good news of God's offer of reconciliation is communicated.

God has entrusted to us a high calling with a high message on His behalf. Our job is to tell earth where heaven stands and what heaven has said, through the presentation of the gospel.

> Therefore, we are ambassadors for Christ, as though God were making an appeal through us; we beg you on behalf of Christ, be reconciled to God. He made Him who knew no sin *to be* sin on our behalf, so that we might become the righteousness of God in Him. (2 Cor. 5:20–21)

Most people do not understand this message. As a result, they spend their time trying to create their own righteousness through religious activities and good works rather than receiving the righteousness that has already been provided through the finished work of Jesus Christ. But God has already reconciled the world unto Himself. God is satisfied with the death and resurrection of Jesus Christ for the payment of sins. The blood of Christ is enough.

Lastly, while not in this order, Paul urged us to share the gospel out of a motivation of *love for God and others*. I have saved love for last due to its overarching theme which weaves itself in and out of the other three motivations.

Jesus modeled this motivation when He preached to large crowds throughout the gospels, as well as when He interacted one on one. The power of His mission came from this motivation of His love for the people He encountered—from Nicodemus, to the blind, deaf, and poor He healed, to his friends Martha, Mary, and Lazarus, to his own disciples. Remember, Jesus came into this world because "God so loved" it (John 3:16).

Jesus models to us that our evangelistic mission is to love the people that God places on our path enough to enter into conversations and relationships that open the way for the good news of the gospel. Not only did Jesus model a motivation of love but so did the apostle Paul. Why was Paul inspired to share the gospel with everyone He encountered? Why was he motivated to travel relentlessly and set up churches throughout the Roman empire—an empire that was hostile to his mission of sharing the gospel? He was motivated out of love for Christ and love for others.

But Paul didn't start out that way. After all, the first glimpse we have of Paul in Scripture is of an angry, driven persecutor of the early Christians (see Acts 7:54–8:3; 9:1–2). Yet Paul's life was completely turned around by an encounter with the risen Christ, and he became convinced of the power of the gospel to change lives—even the life of someone like him who had blasphemed Christ and persecuted His followers (see Acts 9:3–19).

Later in his life, Paul reflected on this amazing transformation marveling that, "It is a trustworthy statement, deserving full acceptance, that Christ Jesus came into the world to save sinners, among whom I am foremost of all" (1 Tim. 1:15). Christ had lavished grace, mercy and patience on this chief of sinners so that Paul would be "an example for those who would believe in Him for eternal life" (1 Tim. 1:16).

Paul is compelled to share this message of God's reconciling love in Christ with others (see 2 Cor. 5:14). So much so, that he says that he, a Jew, so longs for his own Jewish people to know Christ that "I could wish that I myself were accursed, separated from Christ for the sake of my brethren" (Rom. 9:3). Paul could also say that he had expended every means he had in order to bring those he encountered to Christ. We read, "I have become all things to all men, so that I may by all means save some. I do all things for the sake of the gospel" (1 Cor. 9:22–23).

Paul tells us that at the heart of his deep motivation to share the gospel is his own experience of the love of Christ. A lack of passion for the lost is reflective of a lack of love for the Lord. You know how it is when you fall in love: You talk about the one you love. You share photos of the one you love. You include the one you love in what you do and say. Paul's ministry of reconciling others to God mirrored his own encounter with the gospel's reconciling power (see 2 Cor. 5:18). He had personally known the reality of life transformation through God's love. The motivation behind Paul's efforts in evangelism was that he had miraculously been saved, and as a result, he could not help but share the story of his own encounter with the gospel.

WRAPPING IT UP

When we see the full implications of what happens when we accept the gospel and are reconciled to God through Christ, it should motivate us, like Paul, to share the gospel. In fact, you could say that all of the deep theology we find in Paul's letters can be traced back to the reality of Paul's encounter with Christ and his experience with the life-changing power of the gospel.

I have mentioned in earlier chapters that contemporary studies of evangelism show a growing hesitancy on the part of Christians to share the gospel with others. This is a disturbing trend in a time when all of us are seeing the decline of Christianity in our neighborhoods and workplaces. Yet in 2 Corinthians 5, Paul has provided a clear contrast to our contemporary struggle to share the gospel with others in pointing out these four clear motivations for evangelism: the fear of the Lord, power of salvation to transform, ministry of reconciliation, and love of the Lord and of others.

CHAPTER FOUR

THE PRIORITIES

— ◆ —

I was in New York City years ago when a special ceremony was held to honor the firefighters and other rescuers who had put their lives on the line during the terrorist attacks of 9/11. It was a very serious and somber ceremony as the city remembered all those who lost their lives seeking to rescue others on that terrible day.

We have all heard the stories of people who laid aside their own comfort and safety and took great risks to save lives because a lot of people were facing certain doom, and the rescuers knew they could not simply stand by and watch people perish. There was too much at stake to be casual about the situation.

People who are facing certain disaster need a rescuer to lead them out of harm's way, no matter what the cost or inconvenience to the rescuer. And people who are facing certain spiritual disaster without Jesus Christ also need someone to lead them to safety, which is to the cross of Jesus Christ where sin is paid for and forgiven for all those who place their faith in Christ alone. This is why God has called and mobilized the church as a "rescue unit"—to go out into the world and be His witnesses, to turn people on their way to hell toward heaven. "You shall be My witnesses," Jesus said (Acts 1:8).

It is the local church's job, and your job as the pastor, to equip its members to go out among the dying and bring them a message of life. It is our calling as followers of Jesus Christ to lead lost people through the fire and smoke to the safety of the cross. You are never further from the heart of God than when you are silent to your unsaved friends and loved ones about the gospel and the eternal life that Jesus gives. And you are never closer to the heart of God than when you are telling others how they can be saved and bringing them to the Savior. Just as people are trained in CPR so they can rescue people who are in crisis, so the church is God's primary training ground to equip His people in the art of spiritual CPR.

Evangelism is a priority with God. But the problem is evangelism is often not a priority with God's people. One reason is being a witness is not about you and me and what we want God to do for us. It's not about our job, our finances, our children, and so on. In other words, evangelism runs counter to our natural tendency of seeing to our needs first. There is certainly a place for all of the things I mentioned, but being a witness to the world touches the very heart of God Himself.

God has an order within His priority of evangelism. Let's look at what Paul wrote to Timothy, his spiritual son and pastoral representative in Ephesus about this prioritization. In 1 Timothy 2, the apostle laid down key principles for the church that wants to reach its world for Jesus Christ. Notice Paul's emphasis in the opening verses:

> First of all, then, I urge that entreaties and prayers, petitions and thanksgivings, be made on behalf of all men, for kings and all who are in authority, so that we may lead a tranquil and quiet life in all godliness and dignity. This is good and acceptable in the sight of God our Savior, who desires all men to be saved and to come to the knowledge of the truth. (vv. 1–4)

Before we get into the specifics of these and the following verses, please note God desires all people to come to the knowledge of Christ. Peter said of God's desire, "The Lord is not slow about His promise, as some count slowness, but is patient toward you, not wishing for any to perish but for all to come to repentance" (2 Peter 3:9). Our job is to present the gospel freely to all because God's heart is for all the lost which is why He died for all people without exception (see 1 John 2:2; Heb. 2:9).

I'm pointing this out because some Christians give the impression that once they got saved, God went out of the salvation business. I don't know anyone who would actually say that, but Christians who cannot find the time or the concern to share the gospel with anyone else are saying to unsaved people by their actions, "I got my salvation, hope you get yours."

THE PRIORITY OF PRAYER
IN EVANGELISM

So what does the God who wants all people to be saved want His people and His pastors and church leaders to do about it? He wants us to begin by praying for a lost world "first of all" (1 Tim. 2:1). Begin by considering your church's prayer ministry in relation to evangelism. Our biblical calling to *pray* before we go evangelize is sadly lacking in emphasis in the church at large. What is needed in the church today is a renewed understanding that God wants prayer to be at the center of the church's life and evangelistic efforts. In fact, the priority of prayer is such that it should be prioritized before many other programs and projects of the church that, when all is said and done, have an inward, us-centered focus.

The four words Paul used in 1 Timothy 2:1 to describe

prayer are instructive in helping us understand how God wants us to pray evangelistically. The word *entreaties* is related to a word that means "to need" or "to lack," so entreaties are prayers that address a need. What greater need can unsaved people have than their need for Christ?

Next, the word *prayers* is the general word for the act of prayer, and it refers to our worship before God. In fact, this word always points to God when it is used in Scripture. Praying for the lost is an act of worship before God. When the church prays evangelistically, we are bringing people before the throne of God, asking Him to open their hearts.

The third word of 1 Timothy 2:1 is *petitions.* These are requests that we make on behalf of others, which require that we get close enough to people to know what their needs are and feel their pain. And *thanksgivings* simply means to be grateful, which certainly involves thanking God for His saving grace in Christ and for what He is going to do in response to the prayers of His people.

When we put it all together, what God wants from our prayers for evangelism is that we pray for all people, but not just in some general sense of "Lord, I want to pray for the world." Our prayers should reflect our deep concern for the lost as real people and the priority that we have given to their need of Christ.

Many years ago and many pounds ago, I used to be a water safety instructor, the person who trains lifeguards. I became a lifeguard first and then moved on to the water safety instructor position. Let me tell you why I decided to become a water safety instructor. When I was little, I almost drowned. The incident is as real to me today as it was the day it happened, and I can still see it clearly. I was in water over my head and my toes were not touching. I tried to push myself up so I could yell for help, but I was choking on water and couldn't get the word "Help!" out.

The other people in the water might have thought I was playing around, but one person took me seriously and reached into the water to pull me out of what had become a life-and-death situation. After knowing what it felt like to be drowning and have someone deliver me, I wanted to be a deliverer of others so that, if they began to drown, someone would be there for them.

If God has reached down and pulled you out of the miry clay of sin, then you have the responsibility, knowing what it's like to be saved by God, to tell others about how they too can be saved. All of us have the time. The issue is never our busyness, but what is "first of all" in our hearts. What is our priority?

This reminds me of the terrible *Titanic* disaster in which fifteen hundred people drowned in the cold waters of the Atlantic Ocean after the great ship went down in April 1912. Among the many tragic things that happened on that infamous night, one was that many of the lifeboats rowing away from the *Titanic* had room for more people. But those who were safe in the boats didn't want to turn around and go back to save more victims because they were afraid too many people might try to get in and capsize the boats. According to the story, only a few lifeboats turned around and picked up people, when there was room in the boats for many more.

The sinking of the *Titanic* was a tragedy on more than one count. Not only did people die unnecessarily in the water after the ship went down, but you may know that the accident didn't have to happen in the first place. The *Titanic*'s radio operator received a number of messages from other vessels, warning of the danger of icebergs. But none of the messages except the last one was delivered because the radio operator didn't think they were serious enough to be relayed to the captain. So the *Titanic*'s crew didn't know that a life-and-death situation lay ahead of them—and because the message wasn't delivered in time, the ship and those fifteen hundred lives were lost.

It's one thing to try to rescue people who know they are dying. The *Titanic* victims in the water were screaming for help because they knew their lives were ebbing away. But it's just as critical to rescue people who don't realize their danger and aren't even crying out for help. Most lost people in our world are not screaming out for rescue and are drowning spiritually.

I need to ask you some hard questions. Do you have relatives, friends, neighbors, or coworkers on their way to hell today who could legitimately say someday that you never told them about Jesus and how they could be saved? How many people could say to you at the judgment, "I worked next to you for twenty years, and you never told me about Jesus" or "I was family, and yet you never opened your mouth to tell me that I was lost!" It's also important to ask if your church is equipping you to be a spiritual rescuer. If not, something is amiss.

If we really believe Acts 4:12, then there is no excuse for not telling others about Jesus. Speaking of Jesus Christ, Peter said, "There is salvation in no one else; for there is no other name under heaven that has been given among men by which we must be saved." The church needs to be stirred up in the area of evangelism, and the thing that will stir God's people more than any evangelistic "pep talks" or guilt trips or programs is prayer. If you ask me, "How can I get a burden for lost people and overcome my fear of witnessing?" my answer would be to start praying. Pray for unsaved family members, friends, and coworkers by name. Ask God to break your heart over their condition, give you "divine appointments" to share Christ with them, the boldness to speak about Him.

And, by the way, if you feel fearful at times, you are not alone. Even Paul, the great evangelist, asked the Ephesians to pray that he would have the boldness necessary to proclaim the gospel. Paul's prayer request is worth quoting here because it is a great example of how we can pray: "Pray . . . that utterance may be given to me in the opening of my mouth, to make known with boldness the mystery of the gospel . . . that in proclaiming it I may speak boldly, as I ought to speak" (Eph. 6:19–20).

I'm convinced that churches have to do a much more deliberate and thorough job of teaching their members how to pray for lost people and then set the example by making evangelistic prayer a part of the church's regular ministry.

Praying for souls is like holding a magnifying glass over a piece of paper on a sunny day. The glass concentrates the sun's rays on the paper and sets the paper on fire. The glass doesn't increase the sun's power, but focuses it on a particular location. That's what corporate prayer does, which is why prayer is a priority in evangelism.

THE PRIORITY OF PROCLAIMING

Whenever the Bible addresses any subject, it does so with perfect balance. We can see that in 1 Timothy 2. Paul said to begin with prayer for the lost, but he didn't say that this is all the church has to do. In verses 5–7, he drew on his personal example to show that praying for the lost must be accompanied by going to the lost with the good news of salvation. This is what I call "pray-ers"—that is, people who pray—becoming proclaimers.

We have the essence of the gospel in verse 5, where Paul

wrote, "For there is one God, and one mediator also between God and men, the man Christ Jesus." The Word of God tells us that there is only one way to reach God, and that is through Jesus Christ. It doesn't matter if the world thinks the gospel is narrow or intolerant. Scripture says the road is narrow that leads to life. Neither Buddha, Mohammed, nor any other religious figure can bridge the gap between sinful people and a holy God. That chasm from hell to heaven was bridged by Jesus, and only by Jesus, on the cross.

Jesus Christ fits the criteria perfectly because He is both the holy God and a sinless man. Paul continued in 1 Timothy to describe this uniquely qualified mediator: "[Jesus] gave Himself as a ransom for all, the testimony given at the proper time" (2:6). To ransom people means *to pay the price to set them free, to rescue them from their predicament.* He came to rescue people, and if you and I aren't in the rescuing business, we aren't in Jesus' business. He said, "As the Father has sent Me, I also send you" (John 20:21). Where did the Father send the Son? He sent Him into the world to hang out with sinners and bring them to Himself.

Paul knew that his charge to share the gospel involved a combination of prioritizing prayer and proclamation among people. He was glad to say that he was "a preacher and an apostle" (1 Tim. 2:7). A preacher has a message to proclaim, and the word *apostle* means "sent one," so Paul's very job title showed that he was to go out with the gospel. We are not apostles because one of the criteria of being an apostle is having seen Jesus personally, but we *are* "sent ones" because our Savior has commissioned us and sent us into the world with the word of eternal life.

Your priority assignment as a church leader is to be a witness for Jesus Christ first and foremost. And to equip your congregation to be the same. Whether they do so as cleverly disguised salespersons, teachers, physicians, college students, homemakers, or whatever they do—everyone in your church should know their priority is to pray for the lost and proclaim the gospel. If evangelism is far down on your church's priority list, then you shouldn't be surprised if you don't see God showing up in power in your midst. We can't turn God's agenda upside down and expect Him to move among us.

Paul came back to the priority of prayer in 1 Timothy 2:8, where he instructed: "Therefore I want the men in every place to pray, lifting up holy hands, without wrath and dissension." The emphasis here is on those who are leading public prayer in the church assembly. This is a picture of the church at prayer, which Paul said needs to be done with the right attitude because this is not about our private disputes. This verse and verse 1 are like bookends that hold this great section of Scripture together. The church is to pray for all people because God's desire is that all people come to the knowledge of the truth.

WRAPPING IT UP

According to Jesus, "There will be more joy in heaven over one sinner who repents than over ninety-nine righteous persons who need no repentance" (Luke 15:7). If heaven throws a celebration each time a sinner comes to Christ, make sure that you are getting in on the rejoicing by taking someone to heaven with you.

Don't let it be that people you or members of your congregation want to see in heaven fail to make it because you never got around to praying for them and telling them about Christ. Or you never got around to taking seriously your role as a pastor or church leader to teach your congregants about these priorities. It is true, we are not responsible to save people. Only Christ can save. But we can and must be His witnesses. We can pray and go in the confidence that we are putting first things first as God would have us do. And when we act on God's priorities, we can expect His help and His power.

CHAPTER FIVE

THE POWER

◆

Far too often today, when people show up at church, they only do so to relax and enjoy a cappuccino and some cookies. But when the people of the church of the first century showed up, others around them either got really nervous or angry—or they got saved. But either way, when those early disciples showed up, people got shook up.

Whenever Paul came to town, a riot broke out. Right after Paul was saved, he had to leave Damascus hidden in a basket that friends lowered over the city wall late at night to keep his enemies from killing him (see Acts 9:23–25). In Thessalonica, the enemies of Christ mistreated the man in whose house Paul was staying (see Acts 17:5–9). Paul was always starting something, but not because he was a troublemaker. Wherever Paul went, things started to happen because he preached Jesus. He lived and breathed Jesus and expected others to do the same.

The world is ignoring the church these days in a myriad of ways on a myriad of issues. One of the primary reasons is because we are a church without power. Now, I didn't say we are a church without buildings. Nor did I say we are a church without money. It's not that we are even a church without people. But, in many ways, we have become a church without life-transforming and culture-shifting power.

THE HOLY SPIRIT

The Holy Spirit is the power of the church. When our connection to the Spirit is limited, we also limit the power He displays both in and through us to enact true change. In the same way the engine in a car supplies the power to make the car go, the Holy Spirit empowers the church on this mission of evangelism and social impact. By social impact, I am referring *to the good works that church members bring about in the culture at large, affecting positive transformation and witnessing opportunities in whatever sphere the good works occur in.* Without this power source, the church may look good, like a new car sitting in the parking lot. But we won't get anywhere. That's because witnessing to the world without the active participation of the Holy Spirit is impossible.

It is also impossible for the church to be the church that God intended apart from the dynamic ministry of the Holy

Spirit. That's because Jesus said, "Apart from Me you can do nothing" (John 15:5), and Jesus is the One who sent the Spirit to indwell and empower the church.

It was Jesus Himself who alerted us to the absolutely critical role that the Holy Spirit was to play in the church, and it was Jesus who promised to send the Spirit after His ascension back to the Father. On the night before His crucifixion, Jesus told the disciples, "I tell you the truth, it is to your advantage that I go away; for if I do not go away, the Helper will not come to you; but if I go, I will send Him to you" (John 16:7). Jesus then referred to the Spirit as "the Spirit of truth . . . [who] will guide you into all the truth" (v. 13). This is key to the Spirit's ministry.

Now, if you could have taken a vote among the disciples at the Last Supper as to whether they thought it was a good idea for Jesus to leave them, the outcome would have been 11–0, not counting Judas. They didn't want Jesus to leave. They were upset and distressed when He told them He had to leave (see John 16:5–6). And if you asked many believers today which would be better for the church, to have Jesus among us in person or have the Holy Spirit indwelling us, you would probably get a lot of votes for Jesus.

But we are better off with the Spirit than we would be if Jesus were here in the flesh. Jesus limited Himself in the flesh, but the Spirit pervades and invades every place and permanently indwells every believer (see John 14:17b) because He is the omnipresent God, the third Person of the Trinity. It's just that we have failed at not only accessing His power as pastors but also in emphasizing the importance of relying on His power to our parishioners.

Before you go and think I'm pushing it by saying we are better off on earth with the Spirit than with Jesus, keep in mind that Jesus indicated that no Spirit equals no power. Just before His ascension, the Lord made a great promise to His apostles: "You will receive power when the Holy Spirit has come upon you; and you shall be My witnesses both in Jerusalem, and in all Judea and Samaria, and even to the remotest part of the earth" (Acts 1:8). This promise was fulfilled a short time later at the birth of the church in Acts 2.

Think about what Jesus' promise really meant. The apostles had spent more than three years listening to Jesus teach and watching Him work. They had spent three-plus years absorbing truth from the eternal Son of God, who was preparing them to be foundation stones in His church (see Eph. 2:19–20). Peter and the other apostles were not lacking information on what God wanted them to do.

But Jesus knew they were lacking in power. And even though He had been their Bible teacher, He told them that they wouldn't have power until the Holy Spirit came. According to Acts 1:4–5, Jesus prefaced His promise by telling the disciples not to leave Jerusalem until the promised Spirit had been given. Otherwise, all that they had learned wouldn't work. So their main job at that point was to wait for the Holy Spirit to show up.

The disciples did that, and then we read in Acts 2:1–4,

> When the day of Pentecost had come, they were all together in one place. And suddenly there came from heaven a noise like a violent rushing wind, and it filled the whole house where they were sitting. And there appeared to them tongues as of fire distributing themselves, and they rested on each one of them. And they were all filled with the Holy Spirit and began to speak with other tongues, as the Spirit was giving them utterance.

Pentecost was the church's birthday, and it was the power and activity of the Holy Spirit that brought the church into being. The Spirit's presence was manifested as wind and fire, a powerful invasion from heaven that the disciples had never known before.

When the Holy Spirit came with power, the disciples were able to speak in a way they had never been able to speak before, declaring the message of God in a number of languages they hadn't learned (see Acts 2:5–11). They were able to do things they had never done before because they were filled with the Holy Spirit.

What we are missing in the church today is not programs

and seminars and information. We are missing the Spirit's power that comes from His filling. The more Spirit-filled Christians you have in your congregation, the fewer programs you need. The church's job is not to replace the Spirit's ministry with other things, even good things. Having everything in place and being organized is fine, but we have to make sure that we don't organize ourselves out of our need for the Spirit.

Sound Bible teaching is critically important for imparting truth and helping us discern the true from the false when it comes to the claims people make in the spiritual realm. But Bible teaching by itself cannot substitute for the Holy Spirit's presence. Teaching is a prelude to the supernatural. Effective evangelism and social impact cannot take place apart from the Spirit's power.

When Jesus' promise of the Spirit's coming was fulfilled, something supernatural from heaven occurred. The rest of the book of Acts is a proof of Jesus' statement to the disciples that they would receive power when, and only when, the Holy Spirit came and filled them. Acts is about what the local church looks like when the Holy Spirit takes over. Souls were saved. Lives were changed. Communities were improved.

We know that every Christian is indwelt by the Spirit because Paul said, "You are not in the flesh but in the Spirit, if indeed the Spirit of God dwells in you. But if anyone does not have the Spirit of Christ, he does not belong to Him" (Rom.

8:9). The Spirit's abiding presence in the people of God—who make up the church—gives us the continual access to His power that we need to pull off what God has called us to do. We have access to the same power that the Acts 2 church did. As a pastor, that ought to convict you. If you are not seeing radical life change and community impact through your ministry, it may have nothing to do with your preaching. It may have everything to do with the lack of the Spirit's power and presence. After all, God sent the Spirit to interpret the Word to each of us for both our understanding and application (see 1 Cor. 2:9–16).

Jesus made a very interesting statement in John 5:39–40 as He was dealing with those who sought to kill Him (see v. 18). The Lord said, "You search the Scriptures because you think that in them you have eternal life; it is these that testify about Me; and you are unwilling to come to Me so that you may have life." If these people were searching the Scriptures, why wasn't their search leading them to believe in Jesus and find eternal life? One answer is that those who rejected Jesus refused the Holy Spirit's ministry of enlightenment and conviction of the truth (see John 16:8–11).

Jesus' worst enemies, the Pharisees, were what we would call the Bible scholars of the day. They read the Old Testament constantly, but their study led them away from—rather than to—the Messiah. These learned men and their followers had all the right information, but they experienced no transformation because they refused to allow the Holy Spirit to apply His teaching and convicting ministry.

The Bible also teaches that the Holy Spirit is the source of the spiritual gifts that make it possible for the church to execute its ministries of evangelism, discipleship, and social impact. The apostle Paul wrote to the Corinthians concerning spiritual gifts, "Now there are varieties of gifts, but the same Spirit" (1 Cor. 12:4). Going on to verse 7 we read, "But to each one is given the manifestation of the Spirit for the common good." And then after mentioning a number of gifts, Paul clinched his point that the Holy Spirit is sovereignly in charge of the gifts: "But one and the same Spirit works all these things, distributing to each one individually just as He wills" (v. 11). But the Holy Spirit only works where He has the freedom to work through the presence of His filling.

WHO IS FILLING YOU
AND YOUR MEMBERS?

If you and your church are going to be filled with the Holy Spirit, you can't also be full of yourself. All self-centered people can think and talk about is themselves because that's who they care about the most.

Now turn that self-centeredness around, and you have the characteristics of Spirit-filled people. All they can talk and think about is God and what He is doing because He is continuously flowing through them in the power of the Spirit. I love the way Jesus pictured the Spirit's ministry as a constantly flowing stream of water (see John 7:37–39). The Holy Spirit does not want to minister to us in little spurts but as a continuously flowing stream that is constantly refreshing and renewing us. In other words, the Spirit's filling is meant to be a way of life.

If it is this important for us as the church to be filled with the Holy Spirit, the next logical question to ask is how we can get the filling that God commands us to have. God would not give us such a command without telling us how to fulfill it. The question of how to be filled with the Holy Spirit is answered in the three verses that follow the command to be filled with the Spirit given in Ephesians 5:18.

After giving the command to be filled, Paul went on to write, "Speaking to one another in psalms and hymns and spiritual songs, singing and making melody with your heart to the Lord; always giving thanks for all things in the name of our Lord Jesus Christ to God, even the Father; and be subject to one another in the fear of Christ" (vv. 19–21).

Let me summarize these verses. It is in the act and the attitude of worship that believers are filled with the Spirit. A church that wants to be a Spirit-filled church must be a worshiping church. A family that wants to be Spirit-filled must be a worshiping family. And if you want to be Spirit-filled as an individual believer, you must know what worship means and know how to worship.

Worship is the fuel you get at the station when you come to be filled. Worship involves your relationship both with God and with other believers, which is why local church participation is essential for every believer and must be a point of emphasis in your preaching and teaching. This is important because when the Holy Spirit came to indwell and fill the church in Acts 2, the church was gathered in collective worship. The believers were collectively filled with the Spirit again in Acts 4:23–31 as the church gathered to pray for boldness in their witness. The church gathered to worship and went out filled with the Spirit to serve Christ through evangelism and social impact.

I'm not saying that you have to go to church in order to be filled with the Holy Spirit. You can go to church and not be a worshiper. You can go to church, sit back, and let the "professionals" on the stage do your worshiping for you. But having said that, we shouldn't be surprised that the Spirit would grant His filling in the context of the church at worship. The Christian life was never intended to be a solo act. The Bible tells us to sing, not to and for ourselves alone, but "to one another" and to "the Lord."

These things mentioned in Ephesians 5:19–21 are all forms of worship that put us in a dependent position in one way or another. They also require that we reach out to others for their benefit and blessing, not just our own. You see, God is not interested in filling and blessing you just for you. He wants to work through you. That's why the Bible brings the saints into the equation when it talks about the Holy Spirit's filling.

WRAPPING IT UP

Why are so many of us unwilling to become dependent worshipers who yield control of our lives to the Holy Spirit? Our problem is that we don't really believe John 15:5. Jesus said, "Apart from Me you can do nothing." We may quote it, but in the practical sense we don't believe it. Because if we did, we would be falling on our faces before God, asking Him for His filling and His power. We would be praying, "Lord, I am desperate for You because I cannot be the person You want me to be and do what You have asked me to do without the filling and empowering of Your Holy Spirit."

What we as pastors and church leaders need to do is emphasize corporate and private worship as we place ourselves before God and confess our complete dependence on Him as a lifestyle. Worship is a prelude to wielding spiritual power. Because when we do that, the Holy Spirit is free to pour in His filling.

Now you understand why Jesus told the woman at the well that God the Father is seeking people who will worship Him "in spirit and truth" (John 4:23). These are the kind of people on whom God is eager to pour out His power and blessings through the ministry of the Holy Spirit. This is the kind of church God wants us to lead, so we can know the Spirit's power and turn this world upside down for Him, just like the early church did (see Acts 17:6) through evangelism and social impact.

PART TWO

SOCIAL IMPACT

CHAPTER SIX

THE SCOPE

◆

There exists some confusion today about the social implications of the gospel message with regard to our churches today. This confusion has negatively affected the ways churches carry out social impact initiatives, or they're not carried out. As a reminder, the social impact I am referring to involves any good work a believer does which brings glory to God and good to others, within the context of culture at large. Sharing the gospel message of salvation to anyone and everyone is a preeminent role of the church, but limiting the impact of the gospel to content alone reduces our experience in and responsibility to its proclamation.

A lack of attentiveness to the biblical degree that the scope of the gospel includes a mandate of biblical justice in society has kept the church from carrying out its calling of kingdom impact on culture. Some Christians believe that to include social liberation and justice in the gospel is to preach a "different gospel." Others believe that to exclude social liberation and justice as part of the gospel is to deny the (whole) gospel.

To resolve this dilemma, we need to make a distinction between the gospel's content and its scope. This distinction is important because through it is determined the extent that we are to "do justice" as the church as part of our comprehensive responsibility of proclaiming the gospel (Mic. 6:8).

The content of the gospel message is limited and contained. Paul made this unmistakably clear in 1 Corinthians when he said,

> Now I make known to you, brethren, the gospel which I preached to you, which also you received, in which also you stand, by which also you are saved, if you hold fast the word which I preached to you, unless you believed in vain. For I delivered to you as of first importance what I also received, that Christ died for our sins according to the Scriptures, and that He was buried, and that He was raised on the third day according to the Scriptures. (15:1–4)

Clearly, the *content* of the gospel message is the death, burial, and resurrection of Jesus Christ. Scripture is plain that it is personal faith in the finished work of Christ that brings people the forgiveness of sin, a personal relationship with God, and eternal life.

The gospel's *scope*, however, reaches further into sanctification, within which are the concepts of justice and social impact. We see this scope in Paul's use of the word "gospel" when he informs the Christians in Rome that by the "gospel" they are established (Rom. 16:25). The gospel is called "the power of God for salvation" (Rom. 1:16), and is said to include "the righteousness of God . . . revealed from faith to faith" (v. 17). This righteousness includes sanctification, since the righteous shall live by faith (see Hab. 2:4; Rom. 1:17).

In addition, the gospel is viewed as the criterion of Christian conduct, and believers are viewed as being obedient to the gospel when they are active in the ministry of love to poorer believers (see Phil. 1:27; 2 Cor. 9:12–13). Paul further exemplified that the gospel involves more than the initial reception of justification, but also a life of freedom and multiracial relationships when he rebuked Peter for drawing distinctions between Gentiles and Jews on the basis of circumcision. Paul said that in doing so, Peter had not been "straightforward about the truth of the gospel" (Gal. 2:14).

The gospel also encompasses the whole person as directly stated by Paul, "Now may the God of peace Himself sanctify you entirely; and may your spirit and soul and body be preserved complete" (1 Thess. 5:23). A view of humanity that divides the invisible world (soul) from the visible world (body) narrows the understanding of the scope of the gospel. This is reflected in a desire to save people's souls, while simultaneously rejecting or demeaning their personhood and humanity.

This division between the immaterial and material parts of humanity leads to a greater emphasis on the spiritual over the social. However, the biblical relationship of the soul to the body is to be seen as a unified whole. The Hebrew word for soul (*nephesh*) refers to the whole person, which includes the body (Gen. 2:7; Lam. 3:24). In the New Testament, the Greek word for soul (*psuche*) is used to refer to Christ's body, seeing as souls do not die and go to the grave (see Acts 2:27).

Therefore, the church is not only commissioned to deliver the content of the gospel (evangelism) so that people come into a personal relationship with God but also to live out the scope of the gospel (sanctification) so people can realize the full manifestation of it and glorify God. The content of the gospel produces unity in the church as we evangelize the world together. The scope also produces unity through good works that are the basis for social impact.

JESUS AND THE GOSPEL

The greatest illustration of both the content and scope of the gospel is found in Luke chapter 4. This passage took place at a time when the Jews were living in social and economic oppression under Rome. The Jews hated the domination of the Romans, were looking for a Messiah to deliver them, and desperately wanted their freedom.

Jesus was known at that time as a man of no reputation who had been born in a tiny country town called Bethlehem. While news had begun to spread about Him around the other parts of the country, His greatest claim to fame in His hometown of Nazareth was that He was the son of a carpenter.

One day, Jesus returned to Nazareth. As was the custom when there was a visitor, He was given the opportunity to read the Scripture and offer the morning's commentary. Having been handed the book of Isaiah, Jesus turned to the place in Isaiah that He wanted to read. We know He purposefully turned there because Scripture records that He "found the place where it was written . . ." (Luke 4:17). Jesus looked for a particular passage that would deliver a particular truth at a particular time to a particular audience with a particular need. When He found the passage He was looking for, He read,

> "The Spirit of the Lord is upon Me,
> Because He anointed Me to preach the gospel to
>   the poor.
> He has sent Me to proclaim release to the captives,
> And recovery of sight to the blind,
> To set free those who are oppressed,
> To proclaim the favorable year of the Lord."

> And He closed the book, gave it back to the attendant and sat down; and the eyes of all in the synagogue were fixed on Him. And He began to say to them, "Today this Scripture has been fulfilled in your hearing." (Luke 4:18–21)

Don't overlook that Jesus said, "Today this . . . has been fulfilled." The timing of the reading of this passage is crucial. Jesus intentionally chose this passage at a time when the Jews were in the middle of an economic, political, and social crisis. He came on the scene in the midst of a society experiencing the devastating effects of injustice, and said that the Spirit of the Lord was upon Him to proclaim good news: the gospel.

What is essential to note from this passage is that Jesus Himself said that He had good news (the gospel) for those in the economic crisis—the poor. He had good news (the gospel) for those in the political crisis—the captives. He had good news (the gospel) for those in the social crisis—the oppressed.

This good news was the gospel of the favorable year of the Lord. This "favorable year" is also called the Jubilee. To understand it more fully, we need to look at the contextual framework in which it first appeared. We read in Leviticus,

> You shall then sound a ram's horn abroad on the tenth day of the seventh month; on the day of atonement you shall sound a horn all through your land.

You shall thus consecrate the fiftieth year and proclaim a release through the land to all its inhabitants.
It shall be a jubilee for you. (25:9–10)

The year of Jubilee, as noted in this passage, was inaugu-
rated with the Day of Atonement. This was the day set aside
to atone for the sins of the nation of Israel both individually
and corporately. The Day of Atonement was when Israel got
right with God through the shedding of blood—the slaying
of a sacrifice. In other words, they didn't get the Jubilee (i.e.,
God's involvement economically, socially, and politically—
an aspect of the scope of the gospel) without first getting
their sins addressed by God (a type reflecting the future content of the gospel). They didn't get the social until they had
the spiritual. If they skipped the Day of Atonement in order
to get the social benefits of the Jubilee, they lost out on the
Jubilee altogether because there was a prescribed method for
how God instituted His agenda.

A common problem we find in the church today is that a
lot of people want God to do things for them without the Day
of Atonement. A lot of people cry for justice or for God to
pay this, fix that, redeem this, or vindicate that while skipping
the very thing that inaugurates God's Jubilee: the addressing
of personal and corporate sin. God's wrath against sin must
always be addressed, which in the dispensation of the church,
comes through our relationship with Jesus Christ before He

is free to give the social freedom we are looking for. If the spiritual is not foundational, there isn't going to be a Jubilee of social transformation.

The reason that the Jews didn't receive the freedom that Jesus proclaimed to them was that they rejected Him and His atonement. They wanted the social action without the spiritual interaction. However, Jubilee came as the result of the atonement. The other extreme is to emphasize the spiritual while ignoring the issues of justice, equality, racism, sexism, classism, etc. This unfortunately allowed the church to preach about personal salvation for heaven while simultaneously maintaining and promoting injustices on earth.

It is important to note that Jesus proclaimed the good news of the gospel, just like Lady Liberty proclaims her offer for freedom to anyone who has ears to hear in the harbor of New York City. Lady Liberty does not automatically give freedom to someone living in Tibet or Burma any more than she does for someone from Timbuktu. Nor does she force her freedom on anyone who doesn't want it. A person needs to make his or her way to America and go through the process of applying for and accepting what she has to offer in order to bring the proclamation of freedom out of theory and into reality.

Likewise, Jesus proclaimed good news. He proclaimed the gospel. He proclaimed release for the captives and sight for the blind. He didn't force it by eradicating capitalism and developing a spiritualized socialism. He simply offered it under the condition that it must be accepted through a prescribed atonement before it can be experienced.

Jesus couldn't give Jubilee to the Jews because they refused to deal with their sin and receive Him as their Messiah. Jesus would have provided them with the deliverance from Rome they so greatly desired if they had recognized Him as their future atonement and their Lord. However, the Jews wanted the benefits of the Messiah without the relationship with the Messiah. But that's not how God's justice works. No guarantee of deliverance exists without first addressing the spiritual through the atonement.

This is why the church stands poised to be the most effective and most strategic entity in the culture because it is composed of people who are already living and interacting with the spiritual. Not only that, but since Jesus is the fulfillment of the Jubilee in the Church Age, and since it is the responsibility of His body to reflect and extend what He has accomplished (see Eph. 1:22–23), then it is the responsibility of the church, and yours as a pastor or church leader, to manifest Jubilee's liberating principle in history through social impact initiatives.

Many of the Jews witnessed Jesus feeding thousands and healing the sick, but they demanded that He be crucified in exchange for the release of the rebel leader Barabbas. While

Scripture doesn't say their exact motives, many people discern—including myself—that they chose the revolutionary who was attempting to free them from Roman bondage via a revolution, not the One who would do it via the cross. This is because they only wanted social and political freedom, apart from spiritual transformation. They wanted deliverance, but not the King who delivers. And ever since then, mankind has been trying, and failing, to solve the problems of our societies in like manner.

There is a direct correlation between the preeminence given to Christ as King and the freedom a person or a culture experiences. Biblical freedom is the unimpeded opportunity and responsibility to choose to righteously, justly, and legally pursue one's divinely created destiny. To the degree that Jesus is exalted in personal lives, families, churches, and communities is the degree to which the rivers of justice run freely. Jesus' ministry gave the proper order for how to approach all issues of justice and social action. He could have snapped His fingers and delivered all of the poor, the widows, and the oppressed. Instead, He was very particular about His involvement. He became involved in connection with the proclamation of His kingdom message. His purpose was to provide not only physical freedom and relief, but spiritual as well, because He knew that the spiritual and the physical are connected with each other.

Jesus' gospel, as recorded in Luke 4, is the good news that

includes both the spiritual and the physical. To make His proclamation merely social is not good news. If a person has the best food to eat, the nicest clothes to wear, and the greatest job at which to work and yet still dies without a relationship with Christ through His atonement, he ends up not having anything at all.

But to make His proclamation merely spiritual is not the full experience of "good news" either. To tell a person that Jesus can give him a home in heaven, but that He can't do anything about where he lives on earth—or to tell him that he's got shoes, I've got shoes, and all of God's children have shoes in heaven, but that we all have to go barefoot on earth isn't all that good of news either. And while God does not promise to give us everything we want, He does promise to meet our physical needs on earth (see Matt. 6:25–33).

Jesus' gospel includes both the spiritual and the social. It is designed to build God's kingdom rather than try to save the world's systems. It is designed to provide a model of a different system, one created by God, which provides a divine alternative so that the world can see what God can do in broken humanity. All of the social activity in the world cannot solve the world's problems. In the long term, social action is limited; lasting solutions can only come from the kingdom of God because that's where the atonement guarantees lasting freedom.

WRAPPING IT UP

Unless social action is based on spiritual discipleship, it will lack the power for long-term transformation. This is because there is a spiritual reality behind every physical problem. By addressing the underlying theological or spiritual issues, along with the physical, we can achieve long-term solutions because we have addressed the entire problem, not just its physical and social manifestation. Secular society does not understand the spiritual reality that causes physical, social, political, and economic problems. Therefore, secular society is limited in its ability to impact and transform society.

It is the church's responsibility to not only influence culture with the gospel message for salvation in all places and ways we can, but it also involves living out the gospel message in ways that bring God glory and others' good.

CHAPTER SEVEN

THE SALT

◆

The church was established as the mechanism for spreading the gospel and changing the world for the better. It is to be a community of believers whose impact on the culture is greater as a whole than it ever would be individually. But, unfortunately, our churches have often been more focused on building buildings and creating programs than about advancing the kingdom. One of the reasons this has taken place is due to the high regard we have collectively placed on fitting in with our culture.

Yet our identification with Christ as our King automatically brings us into conflict with the accepted values of our culture. The reality of this conflict has become increasingly clear as we have watched the values of our society corrode. Our society is deteriorating spiritually, ethically, and morally. As church leaders, therefore, we must ask ourselves whether we are contributing to the destruction of our culture or bringing the righteousness of Christ to bear on society.

We are living in a nation that has thrown the so-called Protestant belief system out the window—along with the theology that sustained it. People no longer feel obligated to buy into a Christian framework of thinking. This is a deteriorating culture, whether we're talking nationally or locally. People are doing and saying things and espousing ungodly causes that shock us. Or at least they used to shock us. So many of us have become so used to this cultural shift that we no longer are shocked when we experience it.

The problem is compounded when we realize that more is being done in the name of Christ today than ever before. There are more outreach programs and Christian broadcasts, resources and other forms of ministry than ever, yet our culture is not turning around spiritually. Our pastors and our churches have taken on the personality and values of our culture rather than remaining loyal to the King and the Kingdom which we represent. Far too many Christian leaders have lost the zeal for evangelism, along with the follow-up practice of discipleship, while focusing on entertainment and events instead.

Let me illustrate where I'm going by likening our secular culture to a ship. The inhabitants of this ship are the people of our nation, including Christian pastors who lead churches like you and I do. We know from the Bible that this ship is going down someday. In 2 Timothy 3:1–5, Paul says this world will get worse, not better. This cosmos is going to come under God's judgment and be done away with.

But in the meantime, God has put us here, and He has called us to live for Him and display His love and character. So how should we relate to the other people on this ship called culture? Most believers are divided into two primary groups.

THE ISOLATIONISTS

The first group of pastors who lead churches do so in a way that is similar to the isolationists. This brand of church knows that the ship is going down. Those in these churches have read their Bibles. They have their theology straight. They know the ship is going to sink. The others on the ship don't know it, but the isolationists do. So they have decided not to waste time, doing little—if anything—about this doomed vessel. Instead, they want to lower the lifeboat, get into it, and sail off singing the songs of Zion and talking to each other about the impending doom the ship faces.

The isolationists won't have anything to do with the ship. They won't interact with its people, they won't sleep in its cabins, they won't swim in its pool, and they won't play shuffleboard on its deck. They simply separate themselves on the ship because they know it's going down. To a large degree, this group of churches represents one major segment of conservative evangelicalism today. These believers ignore the realities of living in a secular world due to a misguided and misapplied understanding of dispensational theology.

The isolationists meet regularly and smugly in their churches, insisting upon correct doctrine but having little or no contact with the unsaved people around them. Their message is to repent and believe. But because isolationists have so little involvement with the secular culture, very few sinners hear their message and very little social impact is made.

Their approach to evangelism often remains within their own four walls, where everyone is already saved. Or it falls on deaf ears due to a lack of rapport or relevance with others in the culture. Even the movies, music, or free concerts that they make in order to impact the secular culture are so riddled with isolationist verbiage, symbolism, and themes that when they do finally get around to presenting the gospel, their audience is already so highly made up of believers that it's been said that the ones who raise their hands to get saved are doing so for the umpteenth time.

THE CONFORMISTS

But there's a second group of pastors who lead churches who like the ship. I call them the conformists. They enjoy the swimming pool, the plush cabins, and the excellent cuisine.

They get along with all of the crew members and enjoy the benefits of the ship to such an extent that they cannot be distinguished from anyone else on board that sinking vessel. They may not even realize the ship is going down, and if they do realize it, they keep the bad news to themselves or try to live in a state of denial.

This group, in the words of Paul, has become "conformed to this world" (Rom. 12:2). They have become comfortable in Satan's territory. They have been lulled to sleep by American culture's pseudo-Christian atmosphere of baseball, hot dogs, and apple pie. Personal peace and affluence have become their national pastime. Revivals and evangelistic crusades look more like trendy concerts with songs and singers espousing an "inclusionist-gospel"—a gospel that emphasizes inclusion over the gospel itself—linked with those of questionable theology and, some even, with what Paul calls, a "contrary" gospel deserving of being accursed (Gal. 1:8).

So while the isolationists are heralding truth but removed from the world, the conformists are heralding nothing in the midst of it. The results, however, are about the same for each: God's people making little or no difference outside—or inside—the walls of the church. Both groups have missed the biblical mandate. What we need today is a group of pastors who lead churches that are neither isolationists nor conformists, but disciple their members to be God's kingdom citizens who serve as ambassadors to the world. A kingdom citizen is *a visible, verbal follower of Jesus Christ who consistently applies the principles of heaven to the concerns of the culture.*

I mentioned ambassadors in an earlier chapter, but I want to describe it more fully here. What do ambassadors look like? They are *on* the ship called culture, but they are not *of* the ship. They understand that the ship is eventually going to sink. But they also understand that their job is to offer the people an alternative to the options of religious legalism or carnal conformity. God's kingdom ambassadors show this sinking world system what God looks like in its midst.

The church is made up of people who are called to live out heaven's values in the midst of a very hellish world. Living it out is a form of evangelism in and of itself. We receive instructions from above, with our feet firmly planted here below. We are to think heavenly and let it show in our earthly walk. We are looking for the return of Jesus, but we have a lot to do while we're waiting for Him to come.

The measure of any church is twofold: how we grow our members internally and the difference we make in the society externally. It's one thing for your congregants to feel good when they leave the Lord's house on Sunday. But it's another thing for you to equip and inspire them to live from Monday to Saturday in such a way that they influence the community where the Lord's house is located through their witness to the world and their social engagement with the world.

One of the most concise yet comprehensive statements on this subject of how a church is to impact society came from the lips of Jesus in Matthew 5:13–16. In the Sermon on the Mount, Christ used two key metaphors to communicate the impact He wants you and your church to make for Him.

SALT'S PRESERVING INFLUENCE

Jesus told us, "You are the salt of the earth." By declaring us as the salt of the earth, Jesus was making a clear statement about the Christian's role in preserving the decaying condition of this world. Of course, salt has been used as a preservative for thousands of years. Rubbing it into a piece of meat helps to preserve the meat from decay, because salt is an anti-bacterial agent.

Roman soldiers in biblical days were also said to receive some of their pay in salt. The value of salt in a world with no refrigeration was pretty obvious. Salt's value became part of the language, which we can see today in the word *salary*. The word *salary* is actually a derivative of the word *salt*. You're familiar with the expression that "so-and-so is not worth his salt." A person who didn't do his job right didn't receive his full allocation of salt.[1]

---

1. Elizabeth Nix, "Where did the expression 'worth one's salt' come from?," October 15, 2014, updated August 29, 2018, https://www.history.com/news/where-did-the-expression-worth-ones-salt-come-from.

Jesus put His church on earth to act as a preserving influence on the world. If Jesus had nothing on earth for His people to do, He would have taken us out of here the moment we trusted Him as Savior. But, as someone has pointed out, salt can't do its job when it is sitting in the shaker. The church gathered in the house of God is salt in the shaker. When the doors open and we go out into the world is when the shaker is turned upside down to spread the salt of God's Kingdom where it is needed. If our communities are going to be better and souls are going to be saved, then the salt must be at work.

Jesus finished His illustration on salt by saying, "But if the salt has become tasteless, how can it be made salty again? It is no longer good for anything, except to be thrown out and trampled under foot by men" (Matt. 5:13b). In the culture of Jesus' day when salt was so crucial in preserving food, there was nothing worse than salt that had lost its usefulness.

Besides its preserving qualities, salt also creates thirst. As believers gather together in the name of Jesus Christ, the church should make people so thirsty for what we have that they are drawn to Christ like a parched person to water.

I was at an airport one day with some time to spare before my flight boarded, so I went to a little lounge area and ordered a soft drink. The waitress brought me my drink, but she also brought something else I didn't order: a bowl of complimentary salty peanuts. Now you know she didn't do that because the establishment simply wanted to thank me for my business or because they wanted to enhance my airport experience. The only purpose for that salty snack was to dry out my mouth and make me so thirsty that I would open my wallet and say, "Can I have another drink, please?"

The job of the church is to create a thirst in the culture that can only be satisfied by the living water of Jesus Christ. We don't have to worry about trying to make Christianity attractive, palatable, or relevant to the world. All we have to do is make people thirsty for Jesus. And don't forget that when lost people feel their thirst, they will be looking for a thirst-quencher. When Jesus offered the woman at the well a water that would quench her thirst forever, her response was, "Sir, give me this water, so I will not be thirsty" (John 4:15).

THE LIGHT OF THE WORLD

Jesus used a second familiar metaphor in Matthew 5 when He said of His people, "You are the light of the world. A city set on a hill cannot be hidden; nor does anyone light a lamp and put it under a basket, but on the lampstand, and it gives light to all who are in the house" (vv. 14–15).

The last time I checked, the role of light was to shine, and in so doing, to drive back the darkness. The world needs light because it sits in spiritual darkness. We were saved out of that darkness, and now our job is to shine the light of Christ back on the world's darkness. Paul told the Ephesians, "You were formerly darkness, but now you are Light in the Lord; walk as children of Light" (Eph. 5:8).

When we are walking through this world as children of light, the world has a better chance to see things as they really are. "All things become visible when they are exposed by the light, for everything that becomes visible is light" (Eph. 5:13). You know how hard it is to sleep when someone comes in and turns on the light. That's the effect we should have on unbelievers who are sleeping the sleep of eternal death.

If you're in a dark room where people are groping for light, and you know where the light switch is, it's a waste of time to organize a panel discussion on the effects of darkness or shake your head over how terrible the darkness is. Your assignment is to turn on the light, and the darkness will automatically be overcome.

Jesus went on to say, "Let your light shine before men" (Matt. 5:16a). In other words, carry your light where it's dark so that unsaved people can see it. It would be ridiculous to turn on a lamp and then put something over it to hide its glow. If you say you want your house to be a welcoming place on a dark night, it would be foolish to turn the lights on and then close all the curtains so no one can tell you're home.

Yet, all too often, that's what we do in the church. Our lights burn brightly inside the church, but we are the only ones benefiting from them. Meanwhile, the world outside goes on in its darkness. But it's impossible to hide a light that's "set on a hill," and the farther the beam reaches, the more people are affected by it. A local church that wants to measure its effectiveness only has to look into its community to see how far its light is penetrating the darkness. A community that has a church in its midst should be better off because of its presence. Your church must be making an impact in the world around.

Don't misunderstand this—we are not the light itself, but simply the reflector of Christ's light. But God has set the church in the world as a "city on a hill" to reflect His glory. This is what Jesus said in Matthew 5:16. The full verse says, "Let your light shine before men in such a way that they may see your good works, and glorify your Father who is in heaven." We need to talk about the concept of good works. Jesus not only mentioned them here, but Paul said of us, "For we are His workmanship, created in Christ Jesus for *good works*, which God prepared beforehand so that we would walk in them" (Eph. 2:10). God also wants us to be "equipped for every *good work*" (2 Tim. 3:17).

WRAPPING IT UP

So what are the good works you and your congregants are called to do? You are to be the visible demonstration of Christ's love and power within us individually and collectively. Good works are the biblically authorized deeds of kindness, blessing, and social impact that we do to benefit others, in the name of God and for His glory. They are important for the same reason that no one wants a television with sound only. People want a picture to go with the sound. People don't just want to hear us talk about God. They want to see actions that back up our faith.

It's true that unbelievers can build hospitals and orphanages and feed hungry people. But, by definition, the good things that non-Christians do are not done in connection with an authentic relationship with God and His name, and therefore, they are unable to bring Him glory. The good works that we're talking about are based on God's Word and are done to give Him the credit, to shine the light on Him as the ultimate ruler and King. They are also to be done with surpassing excellence and with an intentional goal of presenting the gospel of Jesus Christ.

Everything we do, from our preaching to our service to the community, should bear the stamp of God's character and be worthy of His name and should seek to appropriately bring people into a personal saving knowledge of Jesus Christ. When you live as the salt and light and disciple your members to live as salt and light as well, you will have created a community of believers whose lives are a true witness to the world that promotes justice and righteousness in society (see Ps. 89:14) while simultaneously evangelizing the lost.

CHAPTER EIGHT

THE SOCIAL

◆

As you seek to lead your church and its members into a realm of greater social impact, a thorough understanding of Scripture's view on biblical justice in society will give you the ability to preach and teach on the subject more effectively. This will then inspire your church to do even greater works for God's kingdom. However, *social justice* has become a convoluted term meaning different things to different people.

Biblical justice seeks to protect individual liberty while promoting personal responsibility. For example, the biblical injunction of "Thou shalt not steal" includes areas such as government-sanctioned theft through state-enforced redistribution of wealth and illegitimate taxation.

For our purposes in this chapter, the term I have chosen to use is *biblical justice* rather than social justice because biblical justice provides society with a divine frame of reference from which to operate. The word *justice* in Scripture means to prescribe the right way. Since God is just (see Deut. 32:4) and is the ultimate lawgiver (see James 4:12), His laws and judgments are just and righteous (see Pss. 19:7–9; 111:7–8). They are to be applied without partiality (see Deut. 1:17; Lev. 19:15; Num. 15:16) seeing as justice identifies the moral standard by which God measures human conduct (see Isa. 26:7–8). It is the government's role, then, to be His instrument of divine justice by impartially establishing, reflecting, and applying His divine standards of justice in society (see Ps. 72:1–2, 4; 2 Sam. 8:15; Deut. 4:7–8).

Biblical justice, therefore, is *the equitable and impartial application of the rule of God's moral law in society.* Whether exercising itself through economic, political, social, racial, or criminal justice, the one constant within all four realms (individual, family, church, government) is the understanding and application of God's moral law within the social realm.

It is the division of the sacred and the secular that has led to the cultural disintegration we are now experiencing. It was never the Creator's desire to have such a separation exist in His world. From Genesis to Revelation, it is inextricably clear that the spiritual and the social are always to be integrated if life is to be lived the way God intended.

In fact, the Bible expressly states that the reason there is social disintegration in the form of all kinds of immorality and domestic and international chaos is that man wrongfully segregates the spiritual from the social (see 2 Chron. 15:3–6). When God created man, he was given the responsibility to rule the earth under divine authority while simultaneously displaying God's image to the world (see Gen. 1:26–28). However, it was man's refusal to submit to divine authority that led to the first social disintegration. When man disobeyed God, the result was family breakdown, economic struggle, emotional instability, and physical death (see Gen. 3:1–19).

When God established Israel, He wrote their constitution in the form of the Ten Commandments. These commandments were divided between humanity's responsibility to God and responsibility to his neighbor. Consequently, God deemed the spiritual and social relationship necessary for the proper functioning of society (see Ex. 20:1–17). God also wanted His people to reflect His character through charitable works and acts of kindness to people outside of Israel as a reflection of their gratitude for His goodness to them (see Deut. 10:17–19).

Biblical justice is not a man-made, socially imposed, top-down system ultimately leading to the negation of freedom. Biblical justice promotes freedom through emphasizing accountability, equality, and responsibility in providing a spiritual underpinning in the social realms.

Each of the four jurisdictions in God's kingdom—personal, family, church, and state—is called upon to promote justice and responsibility under God in its own distinct way. Through these jurisdictions, God has given humanity the task of impartially protecting the "unalienable rights" He has granted to each of us. Too many pastors make the mistake of assuming that the church is not a part of the governance in the social realm. And while the church may not have an official role in governing society, it has been tasked with a spiritual role of influencing society through the implementation and support of biblical justice. When the church fails to do this, it becomes so heavenly minded that it is of little earthly good.

BIBLICAL JUSTICE AND THE CHURCH

God's Word is the standard by which the aspects of His law, reflected in truth and righteousness, govern what we do. Who better to understand and proclaim His truths than pastors? Yet we have an absence of pastors and church leaders taking seriously their responsibility to study, apply, and teach principles of biblical justice.

God's justice is predictable because His standard does not change. He does not show partiality in His judgments (see Rom. 2:11; Acts 10:34; Eph. 6:9). He is the righteous judge who renders judgment in equity without regard to status (see Rom. 12:19; Num. 15:16). His instruction given to Moses indicates that humanity is to do the same: "You shall not show partiality in judgment; you shall hear the small and the great alike. You shall not fear man, for the judgment is God's" (Deut. 1:17).

Throughout the Scripture, God has revealed Himself as a defender and deliverer. The Exodus out of Egypt dramatically portrays God's execution of biblical justice on behalf of a group of people who were oppressed. Later, when God gave His laws to Israel, He reminded them of His deliverance. He said, "You shall not wrong a stranger or oppress him, for you were strangers in the land of Egypt" (Ex. 22:21).

God regularly tied either a presence or an absence of biblical justice to a presence or absence of His blessing. For example, Israel's worship was rejected because of an absence of justice in society (see Amos 5:21–24). The Israelites were taken into captivity and held in bondage because of their rebellion against God. God had repeatedly told them to turn from their sin and practice "justice and righteousness," pay back what was stolen, and secure every pledge (see Ezek. 33:10–20). In the destruction of Sodom and Gomorrah, God clearly links His wrath toward them to their lack of concern for the poor (see Ezek. 16:49).

The prophets of the Old Testament regularly condemned the people for their social injustices as well. These social condemnations were not merely viewed as secular affronts to communities but also a spiritual affront to God (see Zech. 7:9–12). God's people were specifically instructed to seek the welfare of the secular city in which they were living and to pray for its wellbeing so that it would become a better place to live, work, and raise their families (see Jer. 29:4–7).

Therefore, the role of the church, as a participant in God's socio-political kingdom and as His bride, is to execute divine justice on behalf of the defenseless, poor, and oppressed. Scripture relates biblical justice distinctly to these groups as a primary concern because it is these groups that most represent the helpless in society and bear the brunt of injustices.

The church is not to mistreat the poor (see James 2:15–16), or to have class and racial prejudice (see Gal. 2:11–14). Rather, the church is commissioned to responsibly meet the physical needs of the "have-nots" within it. Note this is not to be confused with subsidizing irresponsibility, which the Bible strictly prohibits (see 2 Thess. 3:10; Prov. 6:9–11; 10:4; 13:18; 24:30–34). Even in the biblical practice of gleaning—which was leaving behind portions of a harvest for the benefit of the poor who collect it—the poor needed to exercise responsibility in accessing what had been left behind. The amount of work that was put forth resulted in the amount of food that was obtained. The Bible is clear on spiritual ministry and social responsibility working hand in hand. When the two are properly connected and integrated, people become productive citizens of society while also becoming prepared for life in eternity.

A strong biblical connection exists between our knowledge and relationship with God and our concern for the poor and the oppressed (see Jer. 22:16; Matt. 25:34–40). Micah 6:8

reveals this, "He has told you, O man, what is good; and what does the Lord require of you but to do justice, to love kindness, and to walk humbly with your God?" We "do justice" in a humble relation to a just God as a natural reflection of His presence in our lives. Religion becomes authentic when it manifests itself in ministry to others in need.

The second most talked about subject in Scripture, after money, is the poor. More than three hundred verses directly relate to the treatment of the poor, strategies to aid the poor, God's intentions for the poor, and what our perspective should be toward the poor. Space doesn't allow us to go through all of them, but the point is clear that God cares about the poor particularly because they are the most vulnerable to suffering from injustice.

Ultimately, *doing justice* fulfills the two greatest commandments given to us by Jesus—that of loving God and loving others (see Matt. 22:37–40). Christ says, "On these two commandments depend the whole Law and the Prophets" (v. 40). Both the content and meaning of the Law and Prophets were centered not only on one's relationship to God, but also on whether one was rightly related to his neighbor. So having an understanding of and love for God that does not also express itself in love for one's neighbor does not satisfy the biblical definition of love.

Thus, Jesus linked our attitude toward God (spiritual) with our attitude toward others (social). When asked "who is my neighbor?" Jesus responded by telling the story of the Good Samaritan, pointing out that your neighbor is the person whose need you see and are able to meet (Luke 10:26–37). Jesus concludes the story by exhorting us to love in like manner.

It is important to note the meaning of love because we often mistakenly think love is only an emotion. While love can contain emotions, the Greek word used in this command to love others is the word *agapaó* (Luke 10:27).[1] It is not referring to "liking" someone or preferring a certain personality or race. Love is *a choice to compassionately, responsibly, and righteously pursue the well-being of another*. Jesus used the condition of injustice as an intrinsic aspect to a proper perception of defining the meaning of loving one's neighbor. Therefore, since loving one's neighbor includes seeking his best interest by relieving him from injustice or oppression when it is necessary and we are able, love for God is validated through a liberating love for others.

Jesus' earthly ministry to people consistently modeled the integration of the spiritual and the social in that He dwelt among the oppressed (John 4:39–40), ate with them (Luke 5:27–30), comforted them (Luke 12:22–34), fed them (Luke 9:10–17), restored them (Luke 5:12–16), and healed them (Luke 7:18–23) in fulfillment of His Father's will. All of Jesus'

---

1. "agapaó," Strong's Concordance, Bible Hub, https://biblehub.com/greek/25.htm.

good works were clearly connected to the spiritual purposes of God (see Matt. 4:23–24).

The apostle John also stressed the connection between love for God and love for others when he said, "If someone says, 'I love God,' and hates his brother, he is a liar; for the one who does not love his brother whom he has seen, cannot love God whom he has not seen" (1 John 4:20). John reminded us that this love is to be expressed through actions and not just words as it is carried out in "deed and truth" (1 John 3:18).

Further emphasis that this love should be given to the poor and oppressed as special objects of God's concern comes when James writes, "Did not God choose the poor of this world to be rich in faith and heirs of the kingdom which He promised to those who love Him" (James 2:5). He also defines true religion by how one treats the widow and the orphan (see James 1:27).

This same emphasis continued within the operation of the early church. As a result, the influence of the first-century church was so powerful in society that it brought great joy to the entire city (see Acts 8:8) and was said to have turned the world upside down (see Acts 17:6). The church became known for its good works (see Acts 4:32–35; 5:11–16). Members of the church were taught to do good not only to other church members but to all people (see Gal. 6:10).

WRAPPING IT UP

Biblical justice isn't simply a ministry to be relegated to a special event. Biblical justice is a foundational part of fulfilling your witness to the world as a church, reflecting the heart of God.

The social without the spiritual may help people in time but leave them impoverished for eternity. The spiritual without the social may have people looking forward to a great eternity but missing what God wants to do *to*, *through*, and *for* people in history. Both are essential for the transformation of individuals, families, and churches, and our nation.

The church is in the unique position of implementing biblical justice in communities in desperate need of an alternative. Much can be accomplished when like-minded individuals embrace one another's strengths to work together toward a shared kingdom vision of social impact.

CHAPTER NINE

THE SACRED

———————— ◆ ————————

Churches led by pastors who effectively merge the social and the sacred leave a social footprint wherever they are. We've already looked at the role of prayer with regard to evangelism, but it also plays a critical role with regard to social impact. Let me show you a perfect example of what I'm talking about in the person of Nehemiah.

In Nehemiah 1, we learn that this man was a Jewish exile serving in the court of Artaxerxes, King of Persia. Nehemiah heard about the broken-down condition of Jerusalem, and he mourned over the city where God's name dwelt.

But Nehemiah also knew how to strategically engage the spiritual battle at hand through prayer, so in verses 4–11, he went before God in intense prayer. He called on God's name, coming humbly with fasting. He repented of his sins and the sins of his people, and he sought God's forgiveness and healing for the land of Israel. Notice how his prayer ended in verse 11:

"O Lord, I beseech You, may Your ear be attentive to the prayer of Your servant and the prayer of Your servants who delight to revere Your name, and make Your servant successful today and grant him compassion before this man."

"This man," of course, was King Artaxerxes. Nehemiah could pray for success because things were now in proper connection. As soon as Nehemiah said amen, he realized that he was "cupbearer to the king" (v. 11). While it doesn't say so specifically in Scripture, I think that it may have suddenly dawned on Nehemiah that God had already positioned him to make a difference for his people. That was important because Nehemiah was about to go before the king and make an astounding request. He was getting ready to ask permission to go back and rebuild Jerusalem.

Up to this point, Nehemiah had not leveraged his position as the king's cupbearer on behalf of the plight of Jerusalem. But now he set about to utilize what history has proven to be one of the most strategic positions possible. King Artaxerxes was an unsaved and unregenerate man, but he had the power to solve Jerusalem's problem.

A person in Nehemiah's position didn't normally ask for

time off to go and take care of personal business. As the king's cupbearer, he was the king's executive administrative assistant. He also was the one who tasted the king's wine and food before the king got it so no one would try to poison him. Nehemiah was someone King Artaxerxes had learned to trust and rely on. The king wasn't going to let him just disappear for months or even years. But this wasn't a normal situation. Nehemiah had prayed and sought God for his land, and he was willing to put his career on the line to make an impact for God.

Here is a fundamental flaw that has characterized the followers of Jesus Christ, as well as those who preach and teach the corporate body of Christ. We have separated the concept of a career from the act of worship and service to impact the society for the kingdom of God. Many of us have not seen, nor preached on, the kingdom connections among the God we worship, the needs of our culture, and the skills He has given us that we may already be using in our jobs.

Nehemiah's question was how to get the power of Artaxerxes to the people who needed it in Jerusalem. God had already provided the answer by making Nehemiah the king's cupbearer as his career. I don't think it has occurred to many Christians that God has strategically positioned them to affect their culture for Him. One of the things we need to do to rebuild our culture through collective social impact is to "kingdomize" our skills—that is, discover how God can use our so-called secular skills for sacred purposes. God is not limited in the means He can use for a church to make a social impact once His people get lined up behind His purposes. Your congregant's position of influence may extend to your family, your community, and the entire nation.

For example, when Dallas underwent a major social crisis due to the brutal murders of five police officers in 2016, one of the members of the church where I pastor was Chief of police. In fact, Chief Brown was not only a long-standing member of the church, but he had also been listening to my sermons on the radio since he was in college. As a friend, he shared with me later how those messages strengthened him with wisdom to know how to rise to the calling he had of uniting a torn city during a time of chaos and divide. Chief Brown's measured and compassionate response to the ambush and its aftereffects thrust him into an even greater sphere of influence on a national platform. God has used him to spread biblical principles of social justice into our culture at large as well as to give his testimony about his faith in Christ.

Pastor, you do not know how many Chief Browns are in your congregation. It could be a teacher whom God is seeking to use to influence students at school. Or a doctor. Lawyer. Cafeteria worker. Parent. Whomever it is, it is your role to teach truth regarding these delicate issues of biblical justice and the sacred strategy of prayer merged with community involvement. The corporate church should also be involved in compassionately addressing the social, economic, political issues that your community faces from a biblical perspective.

SOME QUESTIONS TO ANSWER

As church leaders, we need to ask ourselves a couple of questions. Are we going to sit and watch our culture fall apart? Are we going to sit and watch our families disintegrate? Or are we going to do something to impact our society for good?

The promise of God's intervention in culture found in 2 Chronicles 7:14 as a result of prayer and humility is an awesome promise, but you can't enjoy this kind of divine intervention with just a little prayer tossed toward heaven now and then. The kind of prayer that will reclaim lives, families, and a nation for God has to take high priority in our schedules. The sacred must merge with the social if the impact is going to be transformative at all.

In fact, if you look back at Nehemiah 1:4, you will see that Nehemiah prayed and fasted for days when he heard about the conditions in Jerusalem. When you want something from God badly enough, you will push other things aside to seek Him for it. He fasted and prayed and sought God, and God revealed His strategy. God was able to reverse years of deterioration in just fifty-two days. We know that God moved in response to Nehemiah's prayer, and used Nehemiah's position of influence to get Artaxerxes to support the rebuilding of Jerusalem. The broken walls were a reflection of the spiritual, social, economic, and political decay that was destroying God's holy city. But Nehemiah didn't start with his position. He started with prayer, which provided the link between God, Nehemiah's problem, and his position.

So let me ask you this personally: If you see something in your life or in your church that is broken, is prayer the first thing you do or the last thing you do? If it's the last thing you do, more than likely, you will have wasted your time on everything else. If prayer comes last, then so will the solution to your problem. God does not like being last. And if the church is going to make a social impact on our world today, we can't afford to keep putting Him last. Some other things are going to have to wait if we are going to turn our communities and nation around. Congregations are going to have to come together in a solemn assembly (Joel 1:14) to repent and to throw themselves before the face of Almighty God. Nehemiah was determined that nothing was going to stop him from seeking God and pleading for His favor.

We could save a lot of time running around and worrying about stuff if we spent time praying and fasting first. You would have to say that, in Nehemiah's case, the crumbled walls of Jerusalem were a major problem, something that cried out for immediate and decisive action. But Nehemiah fasted and prayed first. So my question to you is: What wall is crumbling? The spiritual foundations of this nation are crumbling fast; our beloved nation is imploding upon itself. Political action won't stop the erosion. More money won't stop it. Yet we have a great God who is willing to forgive and heal our land if there are people who are ready to "humble themselves and pray and seek [His] face and turn from their wicked ways" (2 Chron. 7:14). When we do that, He can turn the trajectory of our nation around.

In case I haven't made it clear yet, let me say it right here: The future of our culture and the next generation is squarely in the hands of Christians. Our problem is not just the presence of unrighteousness, but more importantly, it is the loss of God's glory because of it. Unrighteousness and evil have dominated our culture because God's glory has been marginalized, and that marginalization is primarily the result of the removal of Christ's lampstand from the church (Rev. 2:5).

The reason the future of our culture is in the hands of Christians is that the cause of our cultural demise is spiritual. And if a problem is spiritual, its cure must be spiritual. If we are going to make a lasting social impact, we've got to fall on our knees and faces before God and pray. We need to not only talk about prayer, but pray. Not only agree on the importance of prayer, but pray. Not only preach on the power of prayer, but pray. To return our culture to its feet, we must first return to our knees.

2 Chronicles 7:14 is often thrown out as a clarion call for cultural impact through prayer, but the context of this passage is critical in identifying how to employ it as a pastor for

a church. The verse actually begins in the middle of a sentence. So let's set the stage. The occasion is the dedication of Solomon's great temple. Solomon offers a dedicatory prayer in chapter 6 in which he says, in essence, "Lord, I want to lead this people in righteousness. I want to lead this people in honoring You. Lord, I want to do it the way You want it done."

Then, in 2 Chronicles 7:1–10, God's glory came down and filled the temple, and the people offered sacrifices and held a feast. Then the text records:

> Solomon finished the house of the Lord and the king's palace, and successfully completed all that he had planned on doing in the house of the Lord and in his palace. Then the Lord appeared to Solomon at night and said to him, "I have heard your prayer and have chosen this place for Myself as a house of sacrifice. If I shut up the heavens so that there is no rain, or if I command the locust to devour the land, or if I send pestilence among My people, and My people who are called by My name humble themselves and pray and seek My face and turn from their wicked ways, then I will hear from heaven, will forgive their sin and will heal their land. (vv. 11–14)

In this hallmark passage, God calls a nation to pray. Prayer is an earthly request for heavenly intervention. It is the tool and strategy that we have been given in order to pull something down out of the invisible and into the visible. Prayer enacts God's hand like nothing else because prayer is relational communication with God.

Satan's big thing is rendering Christians inoperative. He's not worried about the sinners. He can handle any sinner because the lost already belong to him. But if he can lull Christians to sleep spiritually, he's ready to run the show.

There's a definite posture of heart God is looking for when Christians pray. God's seeking those who will "humble themselves." Humble Christians get through to God. Humility has the idea of dependency. It marks those who understand that, without Him, we can do nothing (John 15:5). Too many of us are autonomous and self-sufficient in our own minds. The Bible calls it being "haughty" because we don't really believe that we need God. God is for emergencies only. We say, "God, don't call me, I'll call You."

And so God allows us to go through trials that we can't fix to humble us and to put us flat on our backs, as if to say, "Now let's see you get up all by yourself." The opposite of God putting you flat on your back is you putting yourself flat on your face before Him in humility.

God says, in essence, "If you want to get My attention, humble yourself. Don't come before Me boastful, proud, and independent because I will let you know you need Me. I do not need you. Humble yourself." Humility is tied to prayer because prayer is, by its nature, an admission of our weakness and need. Many Christians don't pray because they are too proud. Many pastors don't pray because they are too proud.

You say, "But I'm not proud." If you don't pray, you are, because prayer says to God, "I need You. I can't make this church work on my own. I can't solve this problem in our congregation or community on my own. I am not sufficient in myself to do what needs to be done and to be what You want me to be."

Now if God were to stop the rain today or send locusts or pestilence, most of us would form a committee to study the lack of rain. We would get together a commission to do something about the locusts. We would try everything except the one thing that could change the whole thing: coming before God and praying with repentance and obedience.

Unfortunately, too many of God's people have allowed themselves to be shaped and defined by the culture's standards instead of shaping and defining the culture by God's standards. So we wind up giving God what everybody else is giving Him, which is a polite nod. But that won't do. Imagine finding out that your teenager is smoking marijuana because "everyone else I know is doing it." That would not be an acceptable reason. Most Christian parents would say, "So what? You are not everyone else. You are my child, and I didn't raise you that way!"

In the same way, God doesn't want His children conforming to what the rest of the world is doing, adopting their standards. He is saying, "You are called by My name. I'm your Daddy. The rest of the world didn't die on the cross for you. The rest of the world didn't rise from the dead. So the rest of the world shouldn't be telling you what to do."

But the church accommodates the culture. Our culture has redefined morality, commitment, and priorities, and we seem powerless to do anything about it simply because it has become too easy and convenient to adopt its ways as our own.

THE RESULT OF PRAYER

There's an important transitional word right in the middle of 2 Chronicles 7:14. "Then," God says, "I will hear from heaven." That means when we as God's people have fulfilled His conditions and come to Him on His terms, then He will hear us—and not until then.

God says, "If you will come to Me the way that I prescribe, you will have My attention." And more than that, God promises to forgive sin and heal the land when we get His attention. Forgiveness is essential because God is holy. Because of who God is, you can't get past the need for forgiveness. God is distinct from sin. You cannot get God's attention if you go unforgiven. That's why we are told to confess our sins, because God will not listen unless sins are forgiven.

Once God's people are forgiven, then God is free to "heal their land." That is, the effects of their righteousness will spill over first from the church and then to the environment in which they live. This was the way it was supposed to work with Israel. Israel was a special people with a special covenant, and God was to bless all the nations through them. When Israel was right with God, even the Gentiles in their midst were blessed because of their obedience. The healing effects of the promise of 2 Chronicles 7:14 reach beyond individual Christians and even the church to touch the entire society.

WRAPPING IT UP

Christians who are in step with God can use their positions to help transform society. One major reason systems are bad is because the people running the systems are bad. As we move out into society, some of your congregants will be placed in leadership by God, just as Daniel was.

If enough Christians in places of responsibility in medicine, law, government, education, social services, the media, and even the church begin to humble themselves and pray and seek God's face and turn from their wicked ways, we could influence this culture and make the presence of Christ felt from top to bottom and bottom to top. That's what God is after. He wants people who will commit themselves to Him personally and in their churches, and then move out to penetrate the culture for Him through good works and proclaiming the free offer of eternal life through faith in Jesus Christ.

CHAPTER TEN

THE STRATEGY

———————— ◆ ————————

Since the church is the primary manifestation of the kingdom and is the primary means by which God extends His kingdom rule and social impact in this world, local churches must be willing to work individually and across lines in order to become intentional about having a comprehensive strategy that connects both the spiritual and social. Churches must work together to extend their influence beyond their individual walls in order to impact the broader communities they serve.

I have proposed a three-point strategy for invoking a national social impact footprint by the church. This plan involves:

1. A national and localized solemn assembly among churches

2. Community-based good works done collectively for greater impact

3. Churches speaking publicly with one unified voice on the significant cultural issues of our day affecting their communities

SOLEMN ASSEMBLY

God alone sits as the potentate of the universe, saying, as He did through the prophet in Ezekiel 43, "I am the only Savior in town." Therefore, what we need in our nation today is a radical, comprehensive, covenantal return to the God of the Bible—our true and only Savior—and this can be initiated through a collective national solemn assembly in which we seek revival in each of the four kingdom covenantal spheres: individual, family, church, and government.

A solemn assembly for the purpose of restoration is a sacred strategy where God's people, during a specific time of fasting and prayer, seek the renewal of their relationship with Him through the repentance of sin and the passionate pursuit of the return of His presence in their midst. It can also be defined as *a specific move of God, by His Holy Spirit, through His leadership where He gathers the saints to Himself.*

One way of getting a jump-start on this collective impact is by identifying the Christian agencies and individuals who already have intellectual affinity and integration within the spheres of typical American society: education, health care, entertainment, news media, literary, government, business, research, family issues, law, national security, economics, community organizations, and social activism. The primary goal of such identification is to take advantage of opportunities of cross-pollinating efforts while also sharing research on cultural trends and indicators. In doing so, we provide a more synergistic approach to shaping the moral framework of our land.

Some of the goals of this partner-platform might include:

- Awakening and initiating the desire for national revival, personal responsibility, spiritual integration, and progressive reformation.
- Developing a national strategy of social impact, scalable and implementable across cultural, geographical, and class lines.
- Increasing the efficiency and effectiveness of the mobilization and management of Christian resources for national kingdom impact.
- Developing a national ongoing prayer movement to support the initiatives.
- Building and promoting collaboration among churches, nonprofits, training institutions, and agencies.
- Facilitating research and discussion on national trends within the various mediums in order to stimulate strategic influence.

- Reducing wasteful duplication of efforts.
- Creating a forum for the sharing of strategies and techniques while providing responsible forecasting.
- Producing artistically excellent, compelling means of storytelling to encourage kingdom thinking and personal responsibility through mainstream distribution channels.
- Leveraging social media and YouTube to transform thinking toward national renewal and kingdom values.
- Devising a corporate approach to deal with collective felt needs.
- Encouraging thinking about community and national impact as also a local church strategy rather than solely a parachurch strategy.
- Promoting and producing a National Solemn Assembly, drawing together spiritual leaders and laity to seek God's face and invoke His hand in our land.

Over the years and even in the last decade, we have had localized gatherings of believers seeking God's face in order to invoke His hand of involvement in our nation. People have met in cities, churches, and in their homes to call on God and access heaven's intervention in our nation. Many, if not most, of these gatherings lasted one night, one Sunday, or perhaps two Sundays back-to-back. Yet in the busyness of the American lifestyle, it is easy for these experiences to be lumped into another long list of good things to do, and—as a result—lose the collective impact they were intended to have.

Likewise, because many, if not most, of these gatherings occurred segmented by denomination, church, or location, we did not experience renewal on the greater level that it is so desperately needed. Have we gathered as groups to seek God's face in our land? Yes. Have we met in churches every so often and scattered across our nation to seek revival? Yes. But have we ever done this collectively and comprehensively with unity from our nation's spiritual leaders? No. Have we ever done it coupled with the intentional, applicational realities of carrying out God's command of love? Not that I'm aware of.

Lastly, have we truly experienced God's hand of national revival in the last century? I would also argue—no. If we are, as His pastors and His people, going to seek His face—we will need to set aside personal platforms, organizations, denominations, agendas and the like, and come together once and for all as the body of disciples whom Christ died to procure, and call on the name of our great God and King.

Have you ever noticed how special-interest groups in our country carry far more weight in influencing our land (policies, opinions, etc.) even though their numbers are but a small fraction of the number of evangelicals and believers in America? The reason they carry so much weight and influence is because they unite. We may have the numbers in our favor as an overall body of believers, but we rarely prove to be truly united over anything at all.

It is time to set our preferences and egos aside and go before the Lord as one body. It is also time for more than an evening event or Sunday morning assembly. It is time for a comprehensive season of seeking the Lord. One of the ways to do this is to focus an entire segment of time—whether that be a week or several days—on each of the four covenantal areas of God's involvement with humanity: individual, family, church, and society.

Every year in January for the last several decades, I have led our congregation in a weeklong solemn assembly starting on Sunday morning and culminating with a "Break the Fast" breakfast on Saturday morning. This solemn assembly involves giving up some personal physical need or desire every day to call on God for His presence throughout the year. It also involves meeting together as a church body six times in the week, and as individual families one night.

I'm not proposing this as a standard process for carrying out a national solemn assembly, but I am proposing that we enter into something that is more comprehensive and more collective nationwide than a gathering on a Sunday or two. If every serious Bible-believing church would do their own solemn assembly simultaneously with the others—whether that be for a solid week or spread out over four weeks, allowing time for personal reflection during the weekdays—we could seek God as a nation together. If church and organizational leadership would come together in humility and unity, we could actually see the hand of God move in our midst in a way we may have never imagined.

The problem is not merely our waiting on God to involve Himself in our country's demise, but it is also that God is waiting on us to call on Him collectively, according to His prescribed manner.

During its inception, God will often speak to people in separate locations, giving them the similar vision of the need for this type of gathering. When leaders and people meet who may not see each other often, or even know each other, they find that conversations turn to God's movement within their hearts. As a result, synergy arises between denominations and leadership that might not have been there before. And people who may have never worked together across church, denominational, or organizational lines now have their paths cross in this one overarching purpose.

Biblical history is replete with this similar theme of the assembling of the saints and God's subsequent restoration. After all, God has a heart for reconciliation. From the garden in Genesis to the heavens in Revelation, God ushers a call time and again for reconciliation prior to issuing judgment. He is swift to spare, if we will but ask Him for the new heart and the new spirit as His prescribed pathway to seeing hope restored and lives transformed (Ezek. 18:30–31).

COMMUNITY ENGAGEMENT STRATEGY

Another way we can collectively impact our communities and our nation is done through what we have established in Dallas of a local model of church-school partnerships: churches partnering with schools seek to rebuild communities by comprehensively influencing the lives of urban youth and their families in addressing the education, health, economic, and social needs of hurting people based on spiritual principles.

One significant advantage that churches have in being agents of impact for a community is that they are located everywhere. There is an average of three to five churches for every public school in America. Churches are also closer to the needs of the people since they are located in the heart of the community. They also offer the largest volunteer force in the nation. Further, most churches already have buildings to use for community-based programs. By providing a moral frame of reference for making wise choices, churches can equip the community members for social transformation.

One avenue of broadening the churches' impact on their communities is to recognize that churches and schools represent the social, educational, familial, and potentially spiritual nucleus of the community. As people and businesses come and go, churches and schools remain and are ready to accommodate newcomers to their neighborhoods. If these two institutions share common ground as well as longevity, a strategic alliance between the two can precipitate, to a greater degree, positive outcomes for children, youth, and families living in the community.

I remember how this strategy got started organically when I was a young pastor in a predominantly urban community. A nearby high school was experiencing increased difficulties at the time, including delinquencies and low academic achievement. The principal of the school decided to reach out to me for help. Gang activity had broken out, affecting all areas of performance within the school. After I got the call, I decided to go over to the school with around twenty-five men from our church. The principal stopped all the classes and brought all of the male students into the gymnasium, and we shared what it meant to be a mature man.

What's more, we did it in the name of God. In fact, I even used the name of Jesus Christ, and the school was fine with it because, when things have broken down so much that you can't even conduct classes for your students, you don't get so picky about what you will allow or not allow in an effort to help. After our time together, and after some of the men from the church began hanging out in the hallways—offering help and hope to those in need, plus accountability for those who wanted to cause trouble—the gang activity shut down. Student grades went up, delinquency was lowered, and the school acknowledged that the church connection was good for producing a more productive learning environment.

In fact, the principal later became the superintendent of the district of eighteen schools, and requested our church's involvement in all eighteen schools. We then organized ourselves and adopted all of the schools, expanding our support services to each through mentoring, tutoring, counseling, offering skills training and wraparound family support services. When the word got out to neighboring school districts, the eighteen schools soon became thirty-six, and eventually increased upwards of over fifty schools.

One interesting discovery we made in this process was that, in helping the students in the schools, we also gained access to the parents. Many of the problems students had in school were an extension of brokenness in the homes. When we adopted the school, we also connected with the families, which in turn allowed us to connect at a deeper level with the entire community.

Why do we do this? Because the church has been uniquely called to impact our society for good by telling others the good news of the gospel. This starts with the mission of evangelism and then is followed up with discipleship resulting in life transformation on a local and national scale. Changed individuals transform families, and transformed families restore communities.

The church and school partnership initiative strengthens communities and our nation through correcting improper responses to God's Word, which is at the root cause for the dilemmas in society. This successful model has become a national effort through our National Church Adopt-a-School Initiative where we seek, through our national ministry, The Urban Alternative, to train church and lay leaders across the country on how to implement the scalable model in their community. The church and school partnership model exists as a blueprint on how to apply the principles of the kingdom of God while meeting the needs of hurting people through caring interventions underlined with the message of hope.

One of the most exciting aspects of this community outreach strategy is that it is scalable. The program works whether you have a church of forty members or forty thousand. Our church serves more than fifty public schools because we have enough members to sustain that level of impact. However, smaller churches can still make a significant impact in their communities by adopting just one public school.

The ultimate goal of this vision, however, is not the school but the manifestation of God's glory through the power of His body working together to bring about comprehensive change. If every community adopted such a strategy, then over time the whole nation would be impacted through this bottom-up approach to community transformation.

For those pastors of churches who may not want to adopt this specific ministry model, I want to encourage you to implement some form of good works in your community that benefits the broader society and gives an opportunity to share the gospel.

I am living proof that the philosophy behind kingdom community social impact works. The disconnect ended in my own life and family when my father discovered the life-giving power of faith and began operating differently because of it. Our home became different from most of the other homes in my neighborhood because the connection had been made between the spiritual and the social. I am also a product of positive male and female role models from various ethnicities who took the time to mentor and encourage me in such a way so as to propel me further ahead in my life than I may have gone on my own.

This community impact strategy started because I never forgot the transformation that occurred in my own life and family when a spiritual system of belief became the foundation for my decisions. It was then that I saw the link between faith in God and good works for the improvement of my life and the lives of others. In addition, I know the application of this philosophy works because of the thousands of lives that have been transformed through both our local outreach in Dallas and the National Church Adopt-A-School Initiative around the nation.

ONE IMPACT

When the evil citizens of Babel got together to work in unity toward a specific goal in the Old Testament times, God said, "Nothing which they purpose to do will be impossible for them" (Gen. 11:6b). Because of this, God intentionally disrupted their unity through the alteration of the languages they spoke—introducing multiple languages into a people group who had previously spoken the same thing and in the same way.

Far too often in the Christian church today, we come across to the outside culture—and the world—as if we are not even speaking the same language. We don't even look like we are on the same page when it comes to various issues facing our land. Part of the cause of this is because we have neglected to work across denominational and racial boundaries in order to create and pursue a synergistic righteous and biblically sound strategy toward social impact.

When national times of crisis erupt, the church should have a greater collective voice in addressing responses to the chaos. The best way to position ourselves to create and carry out a national plan of restoration involves this three-step strategy—a community-wide solemn assembly, unified social impact, and a shared public voice.

When this is in place, we can speak in unison, calming the anger and hostilities and offering several productive yet strategic options for restoration and justice. Several special-interest groups have been successful in influencing culture because they have managed to unify their collective voice both in the media and entertainment. It is time to set our platforms and personal agendas aside when it comes to the matters of cultural and global importance so that we can effectively speak into and address the concerns of our day. It is time to take our witness and the powerful presence of God's church to the world like never before.

WRAPPING IT UP

When pastors collectively prioritize the process of evangelism and discipleship, massive life-change will occur. This life transformation will then create a ripple effect throughout our land ushering in positive change in society and culture. Evangelism and discipleship serve as the catalyst for all else. When we focus on these two areas as pastors, and when we properly equip our congregants to evangelize and disciple those within their spheres of influence, we will be contributing toward the expansion of God's kingdom agenda on earth.

APPENDIX

——————— ◆ ———————

THE URBAN ALTERNATIVE

The Urban Alternative (TUA) equips, empowers, and unites Christians to impact *individuals, families, churches,* and *communities* through a thoroughly kingdom agenda worldview. In teaching truth, we seek to transform lives.

The core cause of the problems we face in our personal lives, homes, churches, and societies is a spiritual one; therefore, the only way to address it is spiritually. We've tried a political, social, economic, and even a religious agenda.

It's time for a **kingdom agenda**.

> *The kingdom agenda can be defined as the visible manifestation of the comprehensive rule of God over every area of life.*

The unifying central theme throughout the Bible is the glory of God and the advancement of His kingdom. The conjoining thread from Genesis to Revelation—from beginning to end—is focused on one thing: God's glory through advancing God's kingdom.

When you do not have that theme, the Bible becomes disconnected stories that are great for inspiration but seem to be unrelated in purpose and direction. The Bible exists to share God's movement in history toward the establishment and expansion of His kingdom highlighting the connectivity throughout which is the kingdom. Understanding that increases the relevancy of this several thousand-year-old manuscript to your day-to-day living, because the kingdom is not only then, it is now.

The absence of the kingdom's influence in our personal and family lives, churches and communities has led to a deterioration in our world of immense proportions:

- People live segmented, compartmentalized lives because they lack God's kingdom worldview.
- Families disintegrate because they exist for their own satisfaction rather than for the kingdom.
- Churches are limited in the scope of their impact because they fail to comprehend that the goal of the church is not the church itself, but the kingdom.

- Communities have nowhere to turn to find real solutions for real people who have real problems because the church has become divided, in-grown and unable to transform the cultural landscape in any relevant way.

The kingdom agenda offers us a way to see and live life with a solid hope by optimizing the solutions of heaven. When God, and His rule, is no longer the final and authoritative standard under which all else falls, order and hope leaves with Him. But the reverse of that is true as well: As long as you have God, you have hope. If God is still in the picture, and as long as His agenda is still on the table, it's not over.

Even if relationships collapse, God will sustain you. Even if finances dwindle, God will keep you. Even if dreams die, God will revive you. As long as God, and His rule, is still the overarching rule in your life, family, church and community, there is always hope.

Our world needs the King's agenda. Our churches need the King's agenda. Our families need the King's agenda.

In many major cities, there is a loop that drivers can take when they want to get somewhere on the other side of the city, but don't necessarily want to head straight through downtown. This loop will take you close enough to the city so that you can see its towering buildings and skyline, but not close enough to actually experience it.

This is precisely what we, as a culture, have done with God. We have put Him on the "loop" of our personal, family, church and community lives. He's close enough to be at hand should we need Him in an emergency, but far enough away that He can't be the center of who we are.

We want God on the "loop," not the King of the Bible who comes downtown into the very heart of our ways. Leaving God on the "loop" brings about dire consequences as we have seen in our own lives and with others. But when we make God, and His rule, the centerpiece of all we think, do or say, it is then that we will experience Him in the way He longs to be experienced by us.

He wants us to be kingdom people with kingdom minds set on fulfilling His kingdom's purposes. He wants us to pray, as Jesus did, "Not my will, but Thy will be done." Because His is the kingdom, the power and the glory.

There is only one God, and we are not Him. As King and Creator, God calls the shots. It is only when we align ourselves underneath His comprehensive hand that we will access His full power and authority in all spheres of life: personal, familial, church and community.

As we learn how to govern ourselves under God, we then transform the institutions of family, church, and society from a biblically based kingdom worldview.

Under Him, we touch heaven and change earth.

To achieve our goal, we use a variety of strategies, approaches, and resources for reaching and equipping as many people as possible.

BROADCAST MEDIA

Millions of individuals experience *The Alternative with Dr. Tony Evans* through the daily radio broadcast playing on nearly **1,400 RADIO outlets** and in over **130 countries**. The broadcast can also be seen on several television networks, and is viewable online at TonyEvans.org. You can also listen or view the daily broadcast by downloading the Tony Evans app for free in the App store. Over 18,000,000 message downloads/streams occur each year.

LEADERSHIP TRAINING

The Tony Evans Training Center (TETC) facilitates educational programming that embodies the ministry philosophy of Dr. Tony Evans as expressed through the kingdom agenda. The training courses focus on leadership development and discipleship in the following five tracks:

- Bible & Theology
- Personal Growth
- Family and Relationships
- Church Health and Leadership Development
- Society and Community Impact Strategies

The TETC program includes courses for both local and online students. Furthermore, TETC programming includes course work for non-student attendees. Pastors, Christian leaders and Christian laity, both local and at a distance, can seek out The Kingdom Agenda Certificate for personal, spiritual and professional development. For more information, visit: tonyevanstraining.org

The Kingdom Agenda Pastors (KAP) provides a *viable network* for *like-minded pastors* who embrace the Kingdom Agenda philosophy. Pastors have the opportunity to go deeper with Dr. Tony Evans as they are given greater biblical knowledge, practical applications, and resources to impact individuals, families, churches, and communities. KAP welcomes *senior and associate pastors* of all churches. KAP also offers an annual Summit held each year in Dallas with intensive seminars, workshops and resources.

Pastors' Wives Ministry, founded by Dr. Lois Evans, provides *counsel, encouragement,* and *spiritual resources* for pastors' wives as they serve with their husbands in the ministry. A primary focus of the ministry is the KAP Summit that offers senior pastors' wives a safe place to *reflect, renew,* and *relax* along with training in personal development, spiritual growth, and care for their emotional and physical well-being.

COMMUNITY & CULTURAL INFLUENCE

National Church Adopt-A-School Initiative (NCAASI) prepares churches across the country to impact communities by using *public schools as the primary vehicle for effecting positive social change* in urban youth and families. Leaders of churches, school districts, faith-based organizations, and other nonprofit organizations are equipped with the knowledge and tools to *forge partnerships* and build *strong social service delivery systems.* This training is based on the comprehensive church-based community impact strategy conducted by Oak Cliff Bible Fellowship. It addresses such areas as economic development, education, housing, health revitalization, family renewal, and racial reconciliation. We assist churches in tailoring the model to meet specific needs of their communities while simultaneously addressing the spiritual and moral frame of reference. Training events are held annually in the Dallas area at Oak Cliff Bible Fellowship.

Athlete's Impact (AI) exists as an outreach both into and through the sports arena. Coaches are the most influential factor in young people's lives, even ahead of their parents. With the growing rise of fatherlessness in our culture, more young people are looking to their coaches for guidance, character development, practical needs and hope. After Coaches on the influencer scale fall athletes. Athletes (whether professional or amateur) influence younger athletes and kids within their spheres of impact. Knowing this, we have made it our aim to equip and train Coaches and athletes on how to live out and utilize their God-given roles for the benefit of the kingdom. We aim to do this through our iCoach App as well as resources such as The Playbook: A Life Strategy Guide for Athletes.

Tony Evans Films ushers in positive life change through compelling video-shorts, animation and feature-length films. We seek to build kingdom disciples through the power of story. We use a variety of platforms for viewer consumption and have over 35,000,000 digital views. We also merge video-shorts and film with relevant Bible Study materials to bring people to the saving knowledge of Jesus Christ and to strengthen the body of Christ worldwide. Tony Evans Films released our first feature-length film, *Kingdom Men Rising*, in April, 2019 in over 800 theaters nationwide, in partnership with Lifeway Films.

RESOURCE DEVELOPMENT

We are fostering lifelong learning partnerships with the people we serve by providing a variety of published materials. Dr. Evans has published more than 100 unique titles based on over 40 years of preaching whether that is in booklet, book or Bible study format. He also holds the honor of writing and publishing the first full-Bible commentary and Study Bible by an African American, released in 2019.

For more information, and a complimentary copy
of Dr. Evans's devotional newsletter, call (800) 800-3222
or write TUA at P.O. Box 4000, Dallas TX 75208,
or visit us online at www.TonyEvans.org

ACKNOWLEDGMENTS

———————◆———————

I am extremely grateful to the Moody Publishers family for their partnership with me in the development of this series of books for pastors and ministry leaders. Special thanks go to Greg Thornton who has been with me on this publishing journey with Moody Publishers from the start. I also want to thank Heather Hair for her collaboration on this manuscript. I want to acknowledge the Tony Evans Training Center, under the leadership of John Fortner, for the use of some course material which appears in this book. No book comes to life without editorial assistance, and so my thanks also includes Michelle Sincock and Duane Sherman.

TonyEVANS
THE URBAN ALTERNATIVE

Building Kingdom Disciples

At The Urban Alternative, eternity is our priority—for the individual, the family, the church and the nation. The nearly 50-year teaching ministry of Tony Evans has allowed us to reach a world in need with:

The Alternative – Our flagship radio program brings hope and comfort to an audience of millions on over 1,400 radio outlets across the country.

tonyevans.org – Our library of teaching resources provides solid Bible teaching through the inspirational books and sermons of Tony Evans.

Tony Evans Training Center – Experience the adventure of God's Word with our online classroom, providing at-your-own-pace courses for your PC or mobile device.

Tony Evans app – Packed with audio and video clips, devotionals, Scripture readings and dozens of other tools, the mobile app provides inspiration on-the-go.

If you haven't already, get a copy of Tony's Study Bible and Full-Bible Commentary.

tonyevans.org

FREE
EVANGELISM
COURSE!

Go deeper in
your biblical studies
with Dr. Tony Evans. Learn
how to share the gospel with
CONFIDENCE.

MORE FROM
THE KINGDOM PASTOR'S LIBRARY

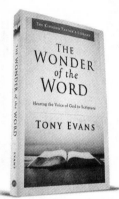
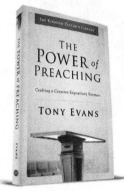
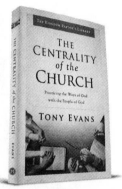

978-0-8024-1831-9   978-0-8024-1830-2   978-0-8024-1832-6

The Kingdom Pastor's Library is a series that brings you a concise, complete pastoral philosophy and training from Tony Evans.

Faithful. Powerful. Practical. Become a Kingdom Pastor today.

also available as eBooks and audiobooks

MOODY
Publishers®

From the Word to Life®

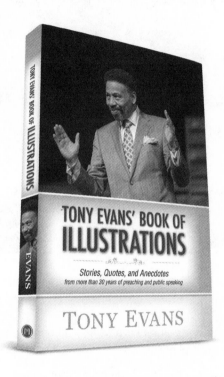